Intersectionality in Health Education

Intersectionality in Health Education

Cara D. Grant, EdD
Troy E. Boddy, DOL

HUMAN KINETICS

SHAPE America

SOCIETY OF HEALTH AND PHYSICAL EDUCATORS®

health. moves. minds.

Library of Congress Cataloging-in-Publication Data

Names: Grant, Cara D., 1977- author. | Boddy, Troy E., 1966- author.
Title: Intersectionality in health education / Cara D. Grant, Troy E.
 Boddy.
Description: Champaign, IL : Human Kinetics, [2025] | Includes
 bibliographical references.
Identifiers: LCCN 2023028837 (print) | LCCN 2023028838 (ebook) | ISBN
 9781718221741 (paperback) | ISBN 9781718221758 (epub) | ISBN
 9781718221765 (pdf)
Subjects: LCSH: Health education--United States--Case studies. | African
 American youth--Education--Case studies. | Culturally relevant
 pedagogy--Case studies. | BISAC: EDUCATION / Teaching / Subjects /
 Health & Sexuality | EDUCATION / Teaching / Methods & Strategies
Classification: LCC RA440.3.U5 G73 2025 (print) | LCC RA440.3.U5 (ebook)
 | DDC 613.071--dc23/eng/20231023
LC record available at https://lccn.loc.gov/2023028837
LC ebook record available at https://lccn.loc.gov/2023028838

ISBN: 978-1-7182-2174-1 (print)

Copyright © 2025 by Human Kinetics, Inc.

The web addresses cited in this text were current as of June 2023, unless otherwise noted.

Acquisitions Editor: Bethany J. Bentley; **Managing Editor:** Anna Lan Seaman; **Copyeditor:** Christina T. Nichols; **Proofreader:** Lyric Dodson; **Permissions Manager:** Laurel Mitchell; **Graphic Designer:** Denise Lowry; **Cover Designer:** Keri Evans; **Cover Design Specialist:** Susan Rothermel Allen; **Photograph (cover):** Hero Images Inc/DigitalVision/Getty Images; **Photographs (interior):** © Human Kinetics, unless otherwise noted; **Photo Asset Manager:** Laura Fitch; **Photo Production Manager:** Jason Allen; **Senior Art Manager:** Kelly Hendren; **Illustrations:** © Human Kinetics, unless otherwise noted; **Production:** Cushing-Malloy, Inc.

Printed in the United States of America   10 9 8 7 6 5 4 3 2 1

Human Kinetics
1607 N. Market Street
Champaign, IL 61820
USA

United States and International
Website: **US.HumanKinetics.com**
Email: info@hkusa.com
Phone: 1-800-747-4457

Canada
Website: **Canada.HumanKinetics.com**
Email: info@hkcanada.com

SHAPE America - Society of Health and Physical Educators
PO Box 225
Annapolis Junction, MD 20701
Website: **www.shapeamerica.org**
Phone: 1-800-213-7193

E9144

Contents

Preface

The concept of **intersectionality** is derived from the 1991 work of Kimberlé Crenshaw (2017), where she unpacked being Black and a woman in terms of racial bias or discrimination and gender bias. Applying the work of looking at the intersections or intersectionality of many marginalized groups in health education can help educators identify and build classrooms where all students see themselves and a dominant narrative does not erase groups of people. Intersectionality can be expanded to any combination of marginalized groups of people—for example, being Latina (Hispanic and female); being an immigrant, dark skinned, and queer; or being poor (low socioeconomic status), homeless, and having a mental health disorder.

This book discusses marginalized groups who identify as "**Black and** …" Some descriptions of intersectional considerations include the following, elaborating on Crenshaw (2017) and Duckworth (2020):

- Largeness in body size as opposed to the slim European ideal put forward in advertising
- Vulnerability to mental health needs
- Neurodiversity
- Sexuality (bisexual, lesbian, pansexual, asexual, gay)
- Ability (some impairment or significant disability)
- Formal education (having little more than high school or elementary education)
- Skin color (dark skinned, different shades of brown or black)
- Citizenship (undocumented or documented immigrant)
- Gender (transgender, intersex, nonbinary, cisgender woman)
- Language (non-English monolingual speaker, learned English)
- Wealth (poor, middle class)
- Housing (homeless, sheltered, renting)

Combining multiple facets of who students are may or may not put them heavily in marginalized categories and groups of people. Historically, marginalized groups are directly limited in access to health care based on social determinants of health. Those who enjoy the most privilege (slim, good mental health, neurotypical, heterosexual, able-bodied, postsecondary educated, white, citizen, cisgender, male, English as first language, rich, and with property ownership) continue to have the most access and are centered closest to access and power (Duckworth 2020).

The goal of this book is to prompt readers to begin having conversations and reflecting on where we are in health education. Start by looking at yourself and identifying where you are in the Wheel of Power and Privilege (see figure P.1). Then take a look at your school district or school data to see where the students you teach are. Overlap the points to see what commonalities you have and what differences are elevated.

Next, consider your health education lesson materials (pictures, scenarios, names used in examples, videos, and other resources) to see if students have the opportunity to share their differences as an asset to the classroom. If they do not, take time to build out structures to get to know students through

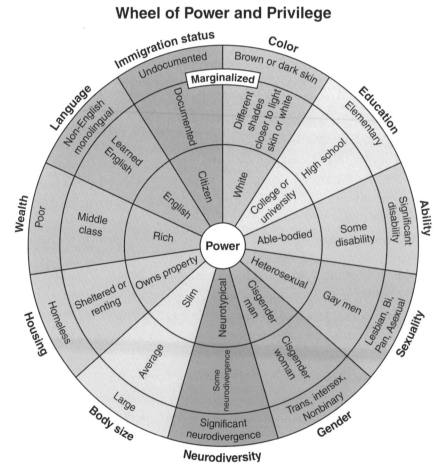

Figure P.1 The wheel of power and privilege.
Courtesy of Canadian Council for Refugees.

relationship building and fostering opportunities for students to add to the narrative presented from a positive angle and not a deficit mindset. For example, are all types of foods from different cultures represented, with ways for students to identify nutrient-dense items within their culture? Are the scenarios pronoun neutral, using *they* or *them* instead of using only binary terms like *she* and *he*? Do you incorporate pictures of students who are large, average, and slim in size in pictures for health? Do you create multiple ways for students to show what they know (i.e., universal design for learning, or UDL)?

Develop equitable calling-on practices where each student has an opportunity to share rather than just the student who always raises their hand or the student you call on to "call out" because you think they are not paying attention. Create a partnership and class environment where all voices are valued and all students feel seen and heard to share their cultural assets with the class—even if they are not the predominant narrative in that school community.

Looking at health education with an intersectionality mindset allows us to consider the complex social influences that will forge progress in how students access health education content knowledge and apply health literacy skills within their own cultural context. As educators, we can develop lesson plans and instructional experiences that (1) consider the experiences and realities of our students belonging to multiple social and cultural identities, while (2) including acknowledgment and critical examination of power and inequality, and (3) incorporating individual and social contexts (peers, school, home, and community) as fluid and dynamic (Else-Quest and Hyde 2016).

The following tables give examples of ways to look at health education content and health literacy skills through the lens of intersectionality.

Sample Health Education Content and Intersectionality

Sample health education content	Intersections
Mental and emotional health	Review neurotypical/atypical cultural norms in accessing mental health care services.
Substance use and misuse	Review data from local police department on how race, gender, age, and sexuality data are collected and who is most at risk for use and misuse.
Nutrition and fitness	Identify various cultures and take a step back from one narrative or monolith.
Safety and injury prevention	Collect data from your geographic area on common injuries and disaggregate data by subgroup (race, gender, age, etc.).
Disease prevention and control	Collect data from the local health department and disaggregate by youth age groups around common illnesses, sexually transmitted infections, cancer, and other noncommunicable and communicable diseases.
Family life and human sexuality	Review various family structures from an asset-based mindset. Be inclusive of differences.

Sample Health Literacy Skills and Intersections

Sample health literacy skills	Intersections
Analyzing influences	Use the Wheel of Power and Privilege points (see figure P.1) to consider how these self-identified points influence health choices: · Largeness in body size as opposed to the slim European ideal put forward in advertising · Vulnerability to mental health needs · Neurodiversity · Sexuality (bisexual, lesbian, pansexual, asexual, gay) · Ability (some impairment or significant disability) · Formal education (having little more than high school or elementary education) · Skin color (dark skinned, different shades of brown or black) · Citizenship (undocumented or documented immigrant) · Gender (transgender, intersex, nonbinary, cisgender woman) · Language (non-English monolingual speaker, learned English) · Wealth (poor, middle class) · Housing (homeless, sheltered, renting)
Accessing information	Identify how and where information is accessed. Does the intersectionality of the individual influence how and where they access information?
Interpersonal communication	Consider cultural norms in communication practices (e.g., communicating peer to peer, student to adult, and student to parent or caregiver).
Decision-making	What influences decision-making based on the points of intersection the student identifies? What are the barriers or limiting factors that may be elevated for or perceived by one group and not another?
Goal setting	How does the goal match the drive within intersectionality?
Self-management	What cultural norms and barriers linked to culture may the student feel regarding self-management? In school, the student is expected to behave a certain way that may be different from perceived norms in their culture. How a student expresses what they know and what learning or instructional processes work for them may not be congruent with the norms in a given teacher's classroom.
Advocacy	How can students reflect on intersectionality to advocate for self, others, and community?

Before moving forward in this book, we want to address how this work originated. The book is made up of case studies, which are rooted in the lived experiences of Black educators, administrators and principals, and higher education professors. The hope of this book is to help others see intersectionality from the viewpoint of being "Black and…" and understand how it creates complexities in access for Black students and educators who learn and teach in systems and institutions that perpetuate and benefit white cultural norms. The case studies provide insight into the lenses, challenges, and opportunities educators face to cultivate more inclusive learning environments for Black students.

Each case study brings readers into a Black educator's classroom to see how they navigate Black students' intersectional lives in the context of health education. While these case studies focus on health education classrooms, it is important to acknowledge that they transpire in all contexts and classrooms. Each case study concludes with key takeaways that the author wants the reader to consider in their practice as well as discussion questions, which can be used for reflection or as a part of a formal discussion.

At the end of the book are two appendixes and definitions for reference. It is essential to work from shared definitions while engaging in conversations focused on race. Additionally, an agreed-upon definition for equity, diversity, and inclusion (EDI) needs to be in place for work to be done with fidelity.

While we value all races and cultures, a multicultural or colorblind approach further separates us from the conversation on race and intersectionality with other marginalized identifiers. Current approaches in health education do not sufficiently disrupt white cultural norms to elevate the distinct experiences of Black youth. This work builds upon Blackshear and Culp's (2023) *Critical Race Studies in Physical Education* and affirms that the Black community has faced unique challenges and hardships—namely, racism—that are embedded in laws, policies, and practices in the United States. Health education teachers who recognize, acknowledge, and accept these unique hardships faced by Black students can awaken their perspective to inquire about and incorporate new practices in health education and work toward identifying, creating, and sustaining equitable learning spaces.

References and Suggested Resources

Blackshear, T., and B. Culp. 2023. *Critical Race Studies in Physical Education*. Champaign, IL: Human Kinetics.

Crenshaw, K.W. 2017. *On Intersectionality: Essential Writings*. New York: New Press. https://scholarship.law.columbia.edu/books/255.

Duckworth, S. (2020). Intersectionality [Infographic]. Flickr. https://flic.kr/p/2jy46K4. CC BY-NC-ND 2.0.

Duckworth, S. 2020. Wheel of Power/Privilege [Infographic]. Flickr. https://flic.kr/p/2jWxeGG. CC BY-NC-ND 2.0.

Else-Quest, N.M., and J.S. Hyde. 2016. "Intersectionality in Quantitative Psychological Research: II. Methods and Techniques." *Psychology of Women Quarterly* 40(3): 319-336.

Nash, J.C. 2008. Re-Thinking Intersectionality. *Feminist Review* 89(1): 1-15. https://doi.org/10.1057/fr.2008.4.

Acknowledgments

This book would not even be a thought, a conceivable idea, without the trailblazing efforts of Tara Blackshear and Brian Culp's work *Critical Race Studies in Physical Education* (Human Kinetics, 2023). Tara and Brian connected us with the dream team at Human Kinetics that fostered the growth and development of this book (Bethany) and the support of SHAPE America's dynamic executive staff and team. We thank these dynamic and courageous authors for telling narratives to break the monolith of Black people by unpacking the many intersections that can further marginalize people.

We would also like to thank our contributors for each sharing their unique voices to provide rich case studies that will engage health educators to think about the complex identities Black students bring to the learning environment. Your enthusiasm for this project was contagious and served as the fuel for us to make it to the finish line.

—Cara and Troy

I am no longer accepting the things I cannot change. I am changing the things I cannot accept.

—Angela Y. Davis, prominent writer, feminist, political activist, and educator

I am extremely blessed and humbled to work on this important project to elevate the voices of others, to identify harm being done, and to share ways to uplift our students and community. My equity journey started so long ago as a person who is multicultural Black and White and who struggles with identity and how this world desires to place us in boxes when we are to be free to be independent thinkers and movers and beings. I am extremely grateful to walk this path with Dr. Troy Boddy, who took up the torch for this work with me and who elevated these conversations years and years ago through work on the equity team in our school district and now beyond the walls to community.

Thank you to Tara and Brian for lifting me up, mentoring me, coaching me to this idea, and giving me permission and encouragement to build upon the great work they started with *Critical Race Studies in Physical Education*.

Thank you to the SHAPE America team, who permit me to share my voice, stay equity centered, and help others see themselves in the journey, and to the EDI podcast team for spreading the word and embracing the difficult conversations. I am grateful for SHAPE Maryland and the team of folks who continue to help me grow personally and professionally in service to others.

I am grateful for my school district family for working with me, calling me out in discomfort, helping me learn and grow, and always lifting up antiracist and antibias work. I am fortunate to be supported by my University of Maryland School of Public Health and College of Education teams, who uplift justice, equity, diversity, and inclusion.

I am thankful for my sorority sisters Rebecca, Kia, and so many more of Lambda Theta Alpha Latin Sorority, Incorporated, who helped me understand and build my own self-efficacy in thinking deeply, questioning, and continuing to be an advocate for the community. It is who we surround ourselves with that elevates us—truly lifting as we climb.

I am thankful for my parents, Rudy and Joanne, who raised me to love all people, no matter their beliefs or differences, and to have a voice even if I got "in trouble" for using it—"good trouble" was always the goal.

To my spouse, Mike, who believed in me, encouraged me, and lifted me up when I felt down or incapable: thank you for loving me unconditionally and being a strong force and drive in my life.

Thank you to our sons, Isaiah, Mike III, Reuben, and Bryce, who are my greatest champions through their pride in me and who drive the fire within me to share stories and to help educators see where harm may be done (unintentionally and intentionally). My goal is that they see the fire and power within themselves and know their worth and value as Black men in our society.

Thank you to all who had a point of influence in my life—to question, to support, to uplift, to help through hardship and so much more!

—Cara

I would like to thank Cara Grant for inviting me to join her for this project. It is a pleasure to work with other educators who are passionate about improving educational outcomes for Black students.

I would like to thank Human Kinetics, specifically Bethany, for working with Cara and me to complete our dream of writing a book that will help educators navigate the rigorous but rewarding process of seeing Black students in their entirety and not through stereotypes and unchallenged assumptions.

To my family and friends, thank you for all the lessons and support you have provided me throughout the years and for always being my biggest cheerleaders.

To my parents, Sue E. Boddy and Ross J. Boddy, thank you for teaching us to always stand up for what is right. I miss you both every day.

To the thousands of students that I interacted with through the years, thank you for being the best teachers and inspirations and for helping me understand that all children can learn when our practices are built on creating inclusive spaces.

To my colleagues at the Sandy Spring Slave Museum and African Art Gallery, thank you for the work you do to educate, elevate, and liberate the community to know the many contributions of Blacks throughout history.

—Troy

"Why Can't You Just Ask for Help?"

Cara D. Grant

Students are greeted at the door as the bell rings for class. Dani sits in her table group and sees the bell ringer (what she is supposed to do as soon as class starts) on the board: "Evaluate health services and determine health services for you in the community." The question is "What are ways you take care of your health each year? Think about what you do to prevent illness." Dani starts brainstorming and writes something about nutrition, exercise, and sleep.

Ms. Jones says, "Today we are going to talk about ways to access valid and reliable health care services in our community." She asks the class to share their responses to the prompt on the board in their table groups before the whole class shares. In Dani's group, Sandi shares something similar to what Dani wrote. José can't think of anything, and James talks about getting a physical to play sports. Ms. Jones opens the discussion up to the whole class and asks the question on the board again: "What are ways you take care of your health each year? Think about what you do to prevent illness." The class shares responses and adds items like going to the dentist, getting physicals every year, and seeing a therapist for mental health care.

Ms. Jones shares that it is important to do preventive care or "wellness visits" each year for health maintenance. Ms. Jones explains, "Your health insurance typically covers these visits so they are affordable. Your parent or guardian can take you to the doctor and dentist. They pay a copay, which makes accessing health care really easy and affordable for you. You go to the doctor at least once a year for a wellness visit and then you go to the dentist every six months to get your teeth cleaned. You don't want to wait until you are sick to go to the doctor. Checking that you are well happens all the time."

Next, Ms. Jones prompts the class to share community resources for wellness visits and how they go to the doctor and ways they access health care in the community. There is a graphic organizer with boxes to complete:

- Who takes you to the doctor?
- Where do you go to the doctor?
- How often should you go to the doctor? To the dentist?
- What are barriers to going to the doctor and dentist?

Dani and her table group fill out the form on their own first and then share with the others in their small group. Dani shares that her mom takes her to the doctor and the dentist, but they don't go every year or every six months to the dentist like Ms. Jones said earlier. Sandi shares that her parents take her to wellness visits annually and to the dentist, but since she has braces for her teeth she also goes to the orthodontist. José does not remember the last time he went to the doctor, but shares that he uses the wellness clinic and has gone to the nurse when he does not feel well. James shares that he just goes to the doctor when he needs a sports physical and thinks he went to the dentist last year, but doesn't remember going twice a year. His dad or his grandma usually takes him. Denise said she goes to a therapist every week for her anxiety and other mental health coping strategies.

Ms. Jones now prompts students to share what they found in their table group reflections with the whole class. She then reemphasizes the importance of going to the doctor every year for a wellness visit and to the dentist twice a year to get your teeth cleaned and checked for cavities. She says, "If you don't do this, you need to determine why and ask your parents to take you because you can have health issues that are not found, and you don't want to wait until you get sick or have a toothache before going to the doctor or the dentist." Ms. Jones does not understand why students would not be able to access health care for wellness visits. They live in an area with plenty of health care options; Ms. Jones simply assumes her students have the same access and opportunities she has.

The students look at each other and are a bit confused. Ms. Jones now prompts students to think of reasons why students responded the way they did in the previous component. Do they have enough opportunities to seek health care, or are there barriers they face? The table group begins talking and sharing their reflections.

Dani says, "I honestly don't know why I don't go to the doctor and dentist that much. I mean, my mom works a lot. Maybe that's why. Maybe it's hard for her to take off from work or the hours don't match up."

Sandi shares, "Hmmm. My mom is super obsessive-compulsive about health care and visits. I think I go to the doctor, dentist, and orthodontist more than I really need to. My mom just flexes or changes her work schedule, and I don't know, I honestly never asked or wondered how she takes off from work or whatever. We just go."

José shares, "I never thought about it before now. When I am sick, we just go to urgent care or the emergency room. One time my grandpa, who lives with us, was sick, and we freaked out and just called for an ambulance to come and get him from our house. It seems like it takes too much time to go to the doctor for all these visits Ms. Jones is talking about. Who has time for that anyway? My parents have to work, and when am I supposed to go when I am at school all the time and then I work on the weekend to help my family out?"

James shares, "I just go for my physical. I don't know what Ms. Jones is talking about with insurance and copay. What is a copay? Because my mom always complains about how much it costs to go to the doctor. I have never heard my mom talk about insurance before … just the bills from the visit."

Denise shares, "I really only go to see my therapist. That takes so much time with seeing them every week. I have not thought about when was the last time I went to another type of doctor. This is stressful. We are just in high school. What's the big deal with all this anyway?"

When Ms. Jones brings the class back together and asks who would like to share barriers for going to the doctor and the dentist, the students are quiet and uncomfortable. She prompts by saying, "You can share what your classmates shared in the small group. It doesn't have to be what you wrote."

With this, Sandi proceeds to share some of what her group shared. "Ms. Jones, our table talked about barriers. Some people can't get their family to take them because of work. They can't take off from work to go to the doctor when it is open, so they just go when they are sick or it's an emergency. Some did not know what you meant by copay. And some had no barriers, but never really talked about it with their parents. They just go."

Ms. Jones looks confused. She grew up going to the doctor regularly; she assumes everyone else does too. She thinks to herself, "Why don't all my students have access to health care? Why can't they just schedule wellness visits and go to the doctor? Why don't their parents care about their health? Don't they all have health insurance? Why would they have barriers?" She honestly just thought her students would say that their barrier was taking time off from school to go to the doctor or the dentist and then she would discuss ways to schedule doctor and dentist visits. She is confused and does not know how to move forward with the conversation, so she just says, "Thank you for sharing, Sandi! Next class we will talk about analyzing influences on our health decisions. Be sure to come ready and discuss how family, friends, social media, and community influence our health. Have a great day, everyone!"

Key Takeaways and Concluding Thoughts

Social determinants of health and the socioecological model illustrate racism as a public health issue in accessing health care for the poor and minorities, which continues structural and institutional racism that is at the core of the founding of this country. As a result, those who are in marginalized groups within the intersectionality model (i.e., race, gender, socioeconomic status, ability level, etc.) have reduced access to health care systems. Within the case study, Ms. Jones illustrated the working assumptions of someone who has privilege and access to health care and is unable to support her students in determining health care services for all in the community. These would include health and human services, local wellness clinics, and wrap-around services by local schools or health agencies for dental, mental, and physical health care, in addition to the services provided for those who have health insurance. Additionally, further investigation and reflection are needed on how Ms. Jones's subconscious racism in providing instruction on accessing health care influences her student's access to health care services.

Discussion Questions

1. What questions could Ms. Jones ask students to help them think of barriers that people might face to getting preventive care in their communities? Why do these barriers exist?
2. What assumptions does Ms. Jones make about health care access for her students?
3. What is the root cause of these assumptions?
4. How does the socioecological model play into access to health care for students?
5. What social determinants are identified in this case study?
6. How could Ms. Jones enhance her lesson plan to provide multiple and varied ways for students to access wellness checkups and preventive care in their community?

Suggested Resources

Braveman, P. 2006. "Health Disparities and Health Equity: Concepts and Measurement." *Annual Review of Public Health* 27: 167-194.

Centers for Disease Control and Prevention. 2007. "The Social-Ecological Model: A Framework for Prevention." Atlanta: Centers for Disease Control and Prevention. www.cdc.gov/ncipc/dvp/social-eco-logical-model_DVP.htm.

CTSA Community Engagement Key Function Committee Task Force on the Principles of Community Engagement. 2011. *Principles of Community Engagement.* 2nd ed. NIH Publication No. 11-7782. Washington, DC: Department of Health and Human Services. www.atsdr.cdc.gov/communityengagement/pdf/PCE_Report_508_FINAL.pdf.

Dahlberg, L.L., and E.G. Krug. 2002. "Violence—A Global Public Health Problem." In *World Report on Violence and Health,* edited by E. Krug, L.L. Dahlberg, J.A. Mercy, A.B. Zwi, and R. Lozano, 1-21. Geneva, Switzerland: World Health Organization.

El-Sayed, A.M., D.W. Finkton, M. Paczkowski, K.M. Keyes, and S. Galea. 2015. "Socioeconomic Position, Health Behaviors, and Racial Disparities in Cause-Specific Infant Mortality in Michigan, USA." *Preventive Medicine* 76: 8-13.

Gee, G., and C. Ford. 2011. "Structural Racism and Health Inequities: Old Issues, New Directions." *Du Bois Review* 8 (1): 115-132.

Hamilton, B.W., J.A. Martin and M.J.K. Osterman. 2016. *National Vital Statistics Reports.* Hyattsville, MD: National Center for Health Statistics.

National Academies of Sciences, Engineering, and Medicine. 2017. *Communities in Action: Pathways to Health Equity.* Edited by A. Baciu, Y. Neguissie, and A. Geller. Washington, DC: National Academies Press. https://doi.org/10.17226/24624.

National Academies of Sciences, Engineering, and Medicine. 2017. "The Root Causes of Health Inequity." In *Communities in Action: Pathways to Health Equity,* edited by A. Baciu, Y. Neguissie, and A. Geller, 99-184. Washington, DC: National Academies Press. www.ncbi.nlm.nih.gov/books/NBK425845/.

National Research Council and Institute of Medicine. 2000. *From Neurons to Neighborhoods: The Science of Early Childhood Development.* Washington, DC: National Academies Press.

Robert Wood Johnson Foundation. 2009. *Beyond Health Care.* New York: Robert Wood Johnson Foundation Commission to Build a Healthier America.

Sabin, J., B.A. Nosek, A. Greenwald, and F.P. Rivara. 2009. "Physicians' Implicit and Explicit Attitudes About Race by MD Race, Ethnicity, and Gender." *Journal of Health Care for the Poor and Underserved* 20 (3):896-913.

World Health Organization. "10 Facts on Health Inequities and Their Causes." 2011. www.who.int/features/factfiles/health_inequities/en.

Williams, D.R., and T.D. Rucker. 2000. "Understanding and Addressing Racial Disparities in Health Care." *Health Care Financing Review* 21 (4): 75-90.

"Don't You All Do That?"

Patricia Morgan

My First Othering Experience

I grew up knowing I was different: a Haitian American born to immigrant parents seeking the American Dream. Everything about me was "exotic"— my accent, my clothing, my hair, my values. I felt it in every room I entered. It was almost as if the air would get tight when I walked in, and I could no longer breathe freely. It was in these moments that I taught myself how to shrink into a less noticeable person. I'm not sure this is what people mean by code-switching, because all authentic aspects of me vanished. **Code-switching** is when a member of an underrepresented group recognizes the power dynamics in the more dominant group and consciously or subconsciously adjusts themselves (i.e., talk, behavior, appearance, dialect, etc.) to gain acceptance, access, or favor so that they can fit into these restrictive and oppressive environments (Doss and Gross 1994). **Assimilation** is when members of underrepresented groups reject or abdicate their core cultural practices and adopt others that are more widely accepted. My feeling embarrassed by my native language and my family's customs and permanently losing that culture was assimilation. I reduced my soul to the smallest pieces of myself so that I could be accepted—so that I could feel loved, valued, and respected.

I am not sure where I learned this from. My island family and friends are very proud people. If you talk to them long enough, you will hear about

Haiti, our beautiful country. Haiti, its name derived from the Indigenous Taíno-Arawak name *Ay-ti*, "land of mountains," was the first Black republic. Haiti was the first country of Black people to free themselves from slavery, and with this comes an indescribable pride. However, that pride was not evident in my day-to-day schooling experience as a first-generation student born to parents who zestfully tried to attain the American Dream. I vividly remember my family telling me stories of their past life in Haiti and sharing the lessons they were taught about their revolution, and I honestly thought they were liars, which I could never say to their faces. I had never seen these stories in my textbooks, and my teachers looked confused when I attempted to share these historical parts of me. I was Haitian American before the hip-hop group Wyclef Jean and the Fugees gained popularity. At that time, it was not cool or hip—it was very lonely.

I wish more people knew how lonely it is to hide parts of you. And not just any parts, but the parts that make you exceptional, the parts of you that are only alive when no one is watching. But for reasons I didn't understand until I was older, I did hide my true self. I reduced myself to someone who talked, walked, ate, and dressed differently, and I even learned how to think differently so that I could be accepted and respected by my grade school teachers and university professors. I became a monolith. A monolith in this context is described as "a large and impersonal political, corporate, or social structure regarded as intractably indivisible and uniform." Yes, "uniform" was me. Dickens and Chavez (2018, 761) say, "Situational factors (e.g., identity) can dictate whether one uses or downplays certain abilities or whether one adopts or suppresses behaviors in different environments." I wanted to blend in so badly that I didn't realize that in doing so, I erased my Black immigrant experience that made me so unique (Kim 2001).

Oftentimes, Black people are seen as a monolith in the United States because of our shared history of enslavement and how our Black skin is perceived by others. And while we do share some customs, norms, and subjection to anti-Black racism on a global level, it's significant to note that we have vastly diverse cultural backgrounds and experiences. Culture represents the accumulated histories, attitudes, behaviors, languages, values, beliefs, and uniqueness that distinguish subcultural groups in a society (Davis 2006; Kroeber and Kluckhohn 1952). It also encompasses a variety of social and sociocultural identity markers such as race, gender, sexual orientation, ethnicity, socioeconomic status, spirituality, disability, and learning differences. However, I was taught a simpler definition of culture that brings it home: "Culture is how we do things around here." And while there are some aspects of culture that are material, external, and observable processes, such as greetings, clothing, language, and celebrations, most of who we are is immaterial, internal, and deep. How I did things in my Black Haitian home was considerably different from how my Black Jamaican friend, my Black Puerto Rican friend, my African American friend, and my Black West African friend did things in their homes. We had very different ways of knowing, doing, and being. Understanding these nuanced experiences is significant in building healthy and authentic relationships.

However, I did not learn about that myself until I moved to Atlanta as a secondary-level teacher in the heart of downtown. At this time, Black people were majority-minority, with over 95 percent of the students classified as Black and 100 percent considered economically disadvantaged. I remember getting my teaching assignment and being elated that I was finally going to work with "my own people." I thought about all the wrongs from my educational past I would make right, how we would have this better bond because they were Black, and how because they were Black I "knew" them. It took less than a month for me to realize that my Haitian Black experience and my students' African American Black experience were two different Black experiences.

It was in that classroom that I learned that we are not a monolith. And it was in that classroom that I learned that I, too, had a lot of unlearning to do about anti-Blackness and my role in supporting oppressive structures (systemic and institutional racism) that reduce us to these uniform beings. **Anti-Blackness** refers to actions or behaviors that minimize, marginalize, or devalue the full participation of Black people in life (Weathersby 2019; Ross 2020). Specifically, it "describes the system of oppression that is based on institutional practices, policies, and cultural messages—as well as the beliefs held by and actions of individuals—to advantage one group over another and is used to oppress Black people" (Jackson 2022, 44).

My first year in Atlanta as a secondary teacher was eye-opening for me. I had so many confrontations with the life I was trying to leave behind. For one, I had to fight against the uniform expectations of being Black. These explicit and monotone descriptions of Blackness were what I had so desperately tried to convince myself that I was—and I tried to impart these expectations on my students. This is where I first learned that I had subconsciously turned into my oppressor. I knew this because I would get a sense of discomfort when my students did not conform to my ways of knowing, being, and doing. My search for success and to attain the American Dream my parents had fought so desperately for me to achieve, I realized, had meant checking certain parts of my culture at the door. My teachers' way of knowing, being, and doing became my way of seeing the world.

Because I had lost touch with my authentic self, I expected my students to do the same. When they didn't conform to my ways, I began to look at them through a deficit-based lens and to use deficit-based language when discussing them during professional team meetings. A **deficit-based lens** is focused on the problem instead of on the potential for greatness. It is thinking of students, families, and communities as projects that need to be solved or fixed. It's shifting the discourse from individual outcomes to systemic barriers that were born from inequitable policies, practices, and, most importantly, deficit belief systems. On the other hand, "**asset-based approaches** utilize the strength and opportunities that the community provides rather than the problems or needs of the community" (Keratithamkul, Kim, and Roehrig 2020, 5).

I even found myself gossiping to my close friend group about how I had inherited this group of undisciplined kids, and it was my job to "fix" them so that they would be ready for the real world. I then realized that because I had survived my cultural cleansing, I thought this instructional method was okay. I thought it was okay for students to check their cultures at the door to gain access to knowledge if it meant there was a sliver of a chance for success. And for this, I am eternally apologetic. We are not saviors sent to erase our students' culture and force onto them the culture of those who would very much like to erase their existence. We are responsible for nurturing their cultural identities and figuring out how to tap into their ways of knowing, doing, and being (Moll et al. 1992). It is our responsibility to embrace the funds of knowledge that students bring to our classes. "Frameworks embracing students' diverse backgrounds and their bank of communal knowledge shows that useful information can be derived from including students' shared community practices into the learning cycle. These banks are commonly referred to as funds of knowledge. Funds of knowledge refer to those historically developed and accumulated strategies (e.g., skills, abilities, ideas, practices) or bodies of knowledge that are essential to a household's functioning and well-being" (Dunac and Demir 2017, 29).

The Stories I Have Seen

Shortly after enrolling in my doctoral program, I was promoted to district-level administrative positions in two different counties. One county had overall similar demographics to what I was familiar with. The other was completely different from my teaching experience and from my school experience as a K-12 student. In the second county, my first placement where I was not a part of the majority, I was in a suburb outside of metro Atlanta. Even though I consider myself a minority as a Black woman in the United States (not globally), I was entering new territory. In this county, I was the first Black woman to assume my role, and the county had previously received legal allegations of racial discrimination from the NAACP. The school district was mainly white, and they were not known for being accepting of diverse cultures and different ways of doing things. The school district prided themselves on "doing things the way it's always been done" because that way was massively successful. After getting in and disaggregating the data, I realized the school district was quite advanced at moving students but only certain types of students: students who were white or

Asian, were middle/upper class, and had limited needs for special services. They, too, thought of academic excellence as a monolith.

Sitting at the administrative level gave me a full view of program effectiveness. It also gave me a different understanding and a full picture of instructional effectiveness. In this role, I found myself challenging long-standing personal beliefs about what an effective teacher was supposed to be based on my training and education. I started comparing my teaching experiences to those of the teachers that I supported. How were they the same, and how did they differ? What would I do if I could go back?

A reflective practitioner constantly finds themself reflecting on practices and challenging past expectations of effective teaching and learning. They also challenge textbook definitions and expectations of positive relationship-building strategies and ways to have meaningful and lasting relationships with their students and community. These reflective moments gave me an opportunity to confront my past—not just as a teacher but also as a student: a student who conformed to the monolithic rules for survival; a student who did not challenge the status quo because she wanted to fit in so badly that she checked not just her culture at the door but also her voice. How would I have advocated for myself had I been brave enough to be me? What would I have wanted someone in a leadership position to do for me? These are the thoughts that ran through my mind as I entered classrooms, as I challenged "the way we've always done things" and made room for new ways of knowing, doing, and being.

The following vignettes highlight my experiences navigating my place in creating safe and affirming spaces for students via their educators, who were oftentimes white women teachers and sometimes weren't; sometimes they looked just like me but held limiting beliefs about children from diverse backgrounds.

Vignette 1: Ms. Tara Brown

I met Ms. Brown in my first year of teaching. We got along almost immediately, and I gravitated to her "tell it like it is" style. She was a strong disciplinarian and taught me a lot about effective teaching and learning and classroom management. She reminded me of my mom in many aspects. She was a powerful, strong, and proud Black woman with a powerful voice. When she spoke, children (and adults) listened.

However, if, by chance, we happened to tour her class, we would sense a cold and monotone culture. The classroom itself was very austere, and within a few minutes, we could tell that students were robbed of their vibrant and colorful personalities. Students were reduced to their previous year's test scores, and Ms. Brown carried an air about her as if students should be grateful for any ounce of structured instruction. Because students were so far behind, it didn't seem that Ms. Brown had enough time to get to know them. She was focused on and always stressed "content before character." Because she had one mission, she didn't feel that students' individuality was of concern to her. In some aspects, she was just like the teachers I had growing up: she voided or separated students from their home culture so that they could fall in line with school culture. In her mind, this was the only imaginable way they could have a chance at success. She justified this treatment because this was how she, too, had learned to survive and succeed in spaces that required her to assimilate.

Most of the lessons she taught me fell in line with the messages I had been fed about being a "good" student. She taught me "not to smile until Christmas" or else the students would think I was weak. She also taught me to plan for "bell-to-bell" instruction to ensure that students were constantly engaged in busy work. She would say, "An idle mind is the devil's workshop." I would be lying if I said these lessons didn't seemingly serve me well during my first couple of months of teaching. Students were afraid of me, and to outsiders my classroom management looked "effective." However, I didn't have meaningful relationships. I had the same relationships with my students as my teachers had had with me. I expected them to fall in line, and if they didn't, they would be subjected to unnecessary discipline, rejection, and othering.

Without realizing it, I had turned into the teachers who erased my identity and cast me to the side when I wouldn't conform to their image of a good student. It didn't matter that Ms. Brown shared a similar skin complexion with our students; she taught them the only tools of success she knew: "If you want to be successful, you have to check your culture at the door."

Vignette 2: Ms. Katherine Horne

Ms. Horne was another teacher I had the opportunity to spend significant time with during my days as a health education, physical education, and science district administrator in a suburban district. Ms. Horne was an older white woman educator who had taught for over 20 years. She could probably teach health and physical education with her eyes closed, and students would fall in line. Ms. Horne considered herself a proponent of diversity and inclusion because she was at one of the more diverse schools in the district.

However, if we took a peek into her physical education teaching spaces and health education classroom, as I did for nearly a decade, we'd see that her students had a different point of view. She treated her students of color as if they were a monolith. She often referenced their liking similar styles of music, fashion, and food. She continued to mispronounce students' names (e.g., pronouncing Jesús as José) even after being corrected and scheduled major physical assignments (e.g., the mile test) on religious holidays when some students had to abstain from liquid and food during daylight hours.

In essence, she also thought of her students as a monolith—a monolith riddled with stereotypes of what Black and Brown students should be.

If we walked into Ms. Horne's physical education or health education class, we would hear mostly hip-hop or reggaeton music. She made assumptions about what types of music her students liked and listened to based on the mere color of their skin. I am certain she never assigned a "getting to know you" survey at the beginning of the school year to ascertain that the group liked this style of music. I often wonder about the rest of the student population who did not enjoy this style and wanted some variety. I am sure some students felt connected to her choice of music; however, I am certain others experienced microaggressions and microinsults in her space because of this behavior. Solorzano, Ceja, and Yosso (2000) describe **microaggressions** as intentional or unintentional commonplace verbal, behavioral, or environmental indignities. And Sue et al. (2007) describe **microinsults** as those behaviors that convey rudeness or insensitivity to a social group or heritage. Both have an unpleasant and negative impact on the psychological safety of the targeted group. In this case, students were unintentionally negatively profiled because of their teacher's assumption about their cultural backgrounds and preference.

The power dynamics of the teacher-student relationship in Ms. Horne's space did not allow a student to speak up. In all honesty, some students may have been sympathetic to her desire to connect with them on a superficial level. However, her intent would never override the impact she made on those students. In her presence, their cultural backgrounds, belief systems, and identities were erased. They became a caricature of what people assumed about their respective cultures. Although she thought she was connecting with them and their culture, she was actually subjecting them to emotional and psychological harm every day they had to come to her class.

Improving Classroom Dynamics Between Teacher and Students

In both vignettes, we experience the cultural invalidations that happen to marginalized groups and students, who often lack safe and affirming spaces to speak up for and be themselves. Irrespective of their own cultural backgrounds, Black, Brown, Indigenous, and other children of color are treated as a monolith, as if the broad array of cultural, ethnic, and linguistic heritage can be summed up in a palatable box of worthiness that is so often associated with the Black, Brown, Indigenous, and other children of color's proximity to whiteness. The way diverse communities deal with othering, mistreatment, and marginalization is also unique and should be considered when approaching methods to dismantle systems of inequities (not giving all students what they need).

Some marginalized groups, such as Asian Americans, have been seen as "model minorities" (Hartlep 2013; Kim 1986), and they are "considered more successful because their values are similar to those of whites, whereas the values of less successful minorities are remote from those of whites" (Kim 1986, 411). However, Asian Americans still experience various forms of discrimination, including acts of random violence amid the COVID-19 pandemic and the use of hateful speech, such as being labeled "forever foreigners" when attempting to settle into American culture (Zhou 2004). Regardless of the cultural differences, all of these marginalized groups continue to be seen as monoliths in and out of the classrooms and encounter dismissive and harmful racialized experiences. The unconscious and conscious stereotypes, prejudices, and biases we carry as educators inform our treatment of students and their lived experiences.

Even if we think the stereotype has good intent—for example, "My students of Asian descent will be great at math/STEM competitions" or "They like to work alone"—it is harmful. Likewise, educators' perceptions of the style of clothes students of color like to wear or the music they like to listen to are just as damaging. These mass assumptions erase students' individuality and educators' opportunity to have meaningful relationships with them. I will not claim that forming authentic relationships with students is easy, because it involves unlearning and relearning ways to fight against the status quo. However, I will provide tools that have helped me develop more authentic relationships with my students and use the curriculum to make impactful changes in their lives.

Strategy 1: Conduct an Authentic Self-Assessment of Biases and Values

Before we can create safe and affirming spaces for others, we need to do so within ourselves. Take time to evaluate how we were socialized in this world and how this socialization has equipped us with long-standing views of others. It is important that this does not become a blame game or a self-pity party. Nothing good results from shame, so it is important that once we realize our biases, we take action to counter the stories we tell ourselves about other people's children. It is also important to note that we all have biases from the diverse ways we're socialized and how we've experienced life. These biases are then reinforced by the systems we are a part of (e.g., schools, church and spiritual settings, and media). It is also important to note that educators and other people of color can have internalized bias, racism, and harmful ideologies about their own group. This work looks different for different folks, but no one is exempt.

Two tools I used to help me in this area were (1) Harvard's Project Implicit Association Tests (IATs) (https://implicit.harvard.edu/implicit/takeatest.html) to uncover some of my hidden biases and (2) Dr. Bobbie Harro's (2000) chapter on the cycle of socialization (see figure 2.1) to better understand the human socialization process and to determine my call to action once I realized change was needed.

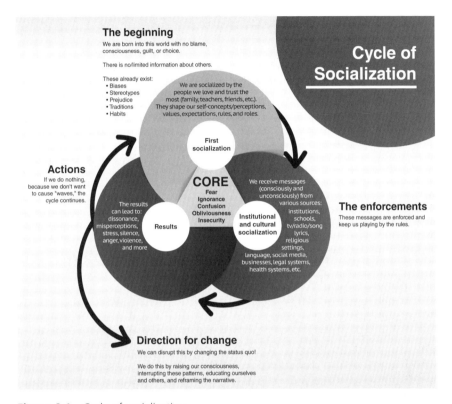

Figure 2.1 Cycle of socialization.

Adapted by permission from B. Harro, "The Cycle of Socialization," in *Readings for Diversity and Social Justice*, edited by M. Adams, W. Blumenfeld, R. Castaneda, et al. (New York: Routledge, 2000), 45-52.

Strategy 2: Increase Cultural Competency and Responsiveness to Various Cultures and How They Are Othered

Oftentimes, we like to pretend that schools are safe spaces away from the violence and hatred that is in the world. However, pretending that the world is safe for children further erases the issues they have to deal with. They don't have the option to ignore the ways they are mistreated. In order to be culturally responsive, we must have an awareness of our own culture, positive attitudes toward cultural differences, and knowledge of the vast array of cultural practices/views that exist, as well as cross-cultural skills to form meaningful and authentic relationships with our students (Banks 2002); Ladson-Billings 1995; Gay 2002). We can't do this with a superficial understanding of our students and their lived experiences. This calls for a commitment to continuously learn and act as we absorb new knowledge. It calls us to challenge our mental models, formed decades before we became educators, and to replace them with better narratives of our students, families, and communities.

Two methods that have helped me do this are (1) relinquishing control of the learning space and focusing on student-centered instruction where students have voice, agency, and choice and (2) focusing on culturally mediated instruction where I find out about my students' cultures (not what I think or assume about their cultures) and ask them to help me embed that into class lessons so it becomes a teachable moment for everyone. This will look different depending on the community, but imagine if we really spent time learning about our students' authentic dance, music, and learning customs. Not only is that a moment for us to learn, but it is also setting the stage for other students to understand the value of being different.

Strategy 3: Support Students in Developing Their Critical Consciousness

Lastly, encourage students to develop their critical consciousness to challenge and change the world. Encourage them to think critically about the issues that are plaguing their communities or their generation and ask them how they want to advocate to make a difference. Health and physical education provides the ultimate space to engage in cross-disciplinary studies of topics that affect their day-to-day lives. No other subject can better show them the interconnectedness of society and how our cultural identities affect everything, including our health and how we move, and give them opportunities to practice health literacy skills. How can we use the curriculum to move students to agency so that it isn't a body of knowledge they are responsible for memorizing and regurgitating but a tool they can use to examine and fight against harmful systems?

Critical consciousness was developed by the Brazilian educator Paulo Freire and colleagues (Freire, Ramos, and Macedo 2014) and is described as "an educational pedagogy to liberate the masses from systemic inequity maintained and perpetuated by process, practices, and outcomes of interdependent systems and institutions" (Jemal 2017). When implemented correctly, it is a form of emotional and psychological armor for our students as they seek to navigate worlds that sometimes ignore them. There are three interconnected parts to schooling for critical consciousness: (1) critical reflection/social analysis—the social analysis and moral rejection of societal inequities; (2) political efficacy/agency—our perceived capacity to effect change; and (3) critical/social action—our individual or collective actions to change policies and practices that are harmful. This can be done via problem-based learning units where students have to engage in inquiry-based projects relevant to their neighborhoods or interests (e.g., addressing characteristics and influential factors of food deserts or elevated air pollution levels in lower-income areas). Next, they can take the information they learned to commit to engaging in social action individually or collectively (e.g., write a letter to their legislator or create a social media campaign to raise awareness).

Two resources that helped me understand critical consciousness better are (1) Freire's (2014) *Pedagogy of the Oppressed* and (2) scholars Seider and Graves' (2020a; 2020b) book *Schooling for Critical Consciousness: Engaging Black and Latinx Youth in Analyzing, Navigating, and Challenging Racial Injustice* and podcast episode of the same title.

Key Takeaways and Concluding Thoughts

As a Black woman educator of Haitian descent, I did not grasp cultural differences and being seen and viewed as the color of my skin immediately. In fact, I spent the better half of my childhood attempting to erase these huge cultural differences so that I could be accepted and celebrated for existing in the manner that was the most familiar, comfortable, and safe for me. I have spent a lot of time unlearning the ways I was conditioned and how I had defaulted to those conditions regarding how best to proceed during confusing times. I can honestly say that I am not at the highest level of cultural proficiency, and I hope to never arrive. I hope I continue to learn and grow in ways that reflect my understanding and society's need for a continuously evolving cultural landscape. I hope I continue to seek knowledge of different cultures and how to best meet students' needs. Not in a manner that shows that students are obligated to teach me but in the humblest way, I can say, "I am here to learn and grow and be better for you." In the words of Lilla Watson (1985), an Aboriginal and women's activist, "If you have come here to help me, you are wasting your time. But if you have come because your liberation is bound up with mine, then let us work together."

In this case study, I, an educator and person of color, shared the pitfalls and challenges of succumbing to institutional and systemic pressures that perpetuate white cultural norms in education that erase other cultures or put them in a monolith. Examples included othering, code-switching, microaggressions in teaching, examples of intersectionality through immigration status (being a person from Haiti)—this is an additional way this concept plays out although not mentioned in this case—and systems of oppression. Harm is being done through consciously or subconsciously continuing practices that keep the systems of oppression going; this looks like a "this is the way we have always done things" culture in schools. Deficit models regarding test scores linked to grouping all people of color into a negative monolith were shared. There was only one right way to do things, and scoring well on tests was the main criterion for success. The deficit model reduces our students that do not "fit in" by focusing on what is different as a problem that needs to be solved or fixed rather than looking at intersectionalities through an asset-based approach that sees in them value added to the classroom. As educators we must focus on our students as assets to and funds of knowledge for the educational process.

Two classroom vignettes highlighted examples more specifically. Ms. Tara Brown focused on test scores and a strict, rigid classroom environment. She cared about content over character and did not focus on relationship building or getting to know her students and how they identified intersectionally. Ms. Katherine Horne unintentionally or intentionally did not value students and showed this by mispronouncing their names, scheduling fitness-based activities on religious holidays when students were fasting, and making numerous assumptions based on her perception of students identifying as people of color. Even though Ms. Brown is Black and Ms. Horne is white, they both did harm through classroom practices, erasing individuality and lumping people into monoliths based on how they present through intersectionality.

Three strategies were shared in the final section. First, conduct an authentic self-assessment of biases and values. This does not point the finger at any particular race or culture, but identifies that educators can and are doing harm to students based on practices they may be completely unaware of. Second, increase cultural competency and responsiveness to various cultures and how they are othered. Get to know students and reflect on making sure that students are not grouped by intersectionality (race, gender, sexuality, sexual orientation, able-bodied or disability status, religion, body size). Lastly, support students in developing their critical consciousness. Once we have developed cultural competency and reflected on practices we may have employed without knowing they could harm others, we help students do the same.

Discussion Questions

1. Lilla Watson, an Aboriginal and women's activist, rejects the idea of people coming to "help" as she fights against inequities and oppression within her community. Considering a critical examination of the social identities we carry, what comparisons can we draw between our own intersectionalities and others?

2. How can we continue to focus on this work while being mindful of the ways we take space/make space for the various ways of knowing, doing, and being?

3. How can we center the experiences of Black, Brown, Indigenous, and other students of color in the classroom and community to ensure their identities are not erased by our standard ways of schooling?

4. Reflect on the different components of intersectionality. What are other possible areas that are often grouped into a monolith or single narrative?

5. Freire, Ramos, and Macedo (2014) state, "There is no such thing as a neutral educational process. Education either functions as an instrument that is used to facilitate the integration of the younger generation into the logic of the present system and bring about conformity to it, or it becomes "the practice of freedom," the means by which men and women deal critically and creatively with reality and discover how to participate in the transformation of their world" (34). How can we use health and physical education curriculum as an emotional and psychological armor to equip students with the tools they need to become change agents?

References and Suggested Resources

Banks, J.A. 2002. *An Introduction to Multicultural Education.* San Francisco, CA: Allyn and Bacon.

Davis, B.M. 2006. *How to Teach Students Who Don't Look Like You: Culturally Relevant Teaching Strategies.* Thousand Oaks, CA: Corwin Press.

Dickens, D.D., and E.L. Chavez. 2018. "Navigating the Workplace: The Costs and Benefits of Shifting Identities at Work Among Early Career U.S. Black Women." *Sex Roles* 78(11-12): 760-774. https://doi.org/10.1007/s11199-017-0844-x.

Doss, R.C., and A.M. Gross. 1994. "The Effects of Black English and Code-Switching on Intraracial Perceptions." *Journal of Black Psychology* 20(3): 282. https://doi.org/10.1177/00957984940203003.

Dunac, P.S., and K. Demir. 2017. "Negotiating White Science in a Racially and Ethnically Diverse United States." *Educational Review* 69(1): 25-50. https://doi.org/10.1080/00131911.2016.1150255.

Freire, P., M.B. Ramos, and D. Macedo. 2014. *Pedagogy of the Oppressed.* 30th anniv. ed. New York City: Continuum.

Gay, G. 2002. *Culturally Responsive Teaching: Theory, Research and Practice.* New York City: Teachers College Press.

Harro, B. 2000. "The Cycle of Socialization." In *Readings for Diversity and Social Justice,* edited by M. Adams, W. Blumenfeld, R. Castaneda, H. Hackman, M. Peters, and X. Zuniga, 45-52. Routledge.

Hartlep, N.D. 2013. *The Model Minority Stereotype: Demystifying Asian American Success.* Charlotte, NC: Information Age.

Jackson, D. 2022. "Making Sense of Black Students' Figured Worlds of Race, Racism, Anti-Blackness, and Blackness." *Research in the Teaching of English* 57 (1): 43-66.

Jemal, A. 2017. "Critical Consciousness: A Critique and Critical Analysis of the Literature." *Urban Review: Issues and Ideas in Public Education* 49 (4): 602-626.

Ladson-Billings, G. 1995. "Toward a Theory of Culturally Relevant Pedagogy." *American Education Research Journal* 32 (3): pp. 465-491.

Keratithamkul, K., J.N. Kim, and G.H. Roehrig. 2020. "Cultural Competence or Deficit-Based View? A Qualitative Approach to Understanding Middle School Students' Experience with Culturally Framed Engineering." *International Journal of STEM Education* 7 (26): 1-15.

Kim, H. 1986. "Model Minority." In *Dictionary of Asian American History*, edited by H. Kim, 411. Westport, CT: Greenwood Press.

Kim, Y.Y. 2001. *Becoming Intercultural : An Integrative Theory of Communication and Cross-Cultural Adaptation*. Thousand Oaks, CA: Sage Publications Inc.

Kroeber, A.L., and C. Kluckhohn. 1952. *Culture: A Critical Review of Concepts and Definitions*. Cambridge, MA: Peabody Museum Press.

Moll, L.C., C. Amanti, D. Neff, and N. Gonzalez. 1992. "Funds of Knowledge for Teaching: Using a Qualitative Approach to Connect Homes and Classrooms." *Theory Into Practice* 31(2): 132-141.

Ross, K.M. 2020. "Call It What It Is: Antiblackness (When Black People Are Killed by the Police, 'Racism' Isn't the Right Word)." *New York Times*, June 4, 2020. www.nytimes.com/2020/06/04/opinion/george-floyd-anti-blackness.html.

Seider, S., and D. Graves. 2020a. *Schooling for Critical Consciousness: Engaging Black and Latinx Youth in Analyzing, Navigating, and Challenging Racial Injustice*. Cambridge, MA: Harvard Education Press.

Seider, S., and D. Graves. 2020b. "Scott Seider and Daren Graves—Schooling for Critical Consciousness: Engaging Black and Latinx Youth in Analyzing, Navigating, and Challenging Racial Injustice." February 3, 2020, in *Principal Center Radio*. Podcast, 35:09. https://principalcenter.podbean.com/e/scottseider-and-daren-graves%e2%80%94schoolingfor-critical-consciousness-engaging-black-and-latinx-youthin-analyzing-navigatingandchallenging-racial-i/.

Solorzano, D., M. Ceja, and T. Yosso. 2000. "Critical Race Theory, Racial Microaggressions, and Campus Racial Climate: The Experiences of African American College Students." *Journal of Negro Education* 69 (1/2): 60-73.

Sue, D.W., C.M. Capodilupo, G.C. Torino, J.M. Bucceri, A.M.B. Holder, K.L. Nadal, and M. Esquilin. 2007. "Racial Microaggressions in Everyday Life: Implications for Clinical Practice." *American Psychologist* 62 (4): 271-286. https://doi.org/10.1037/0003-066X.62.4.271.

Watson, L. 1985. United Nations Decade for Women Conference. Nairobi.

Weathersby, C. 2019. *Anti-Blackness and Public Schools in the Border South: Policy, Politics, and Protest in St. Louis, 1865-1972*. Charlotte, NC: Information Age.

Zhou, M. 2004. "Are Asian Americans Becoming 'White'?" *Contexts* 3 (1): 29-37.

Zhou, M., and A.C. Ocampo. 2016. "Critical Thoughts on Asian American Assimilation in the Whitening Literature." In *Contemporary Asian America: A Multidisciplinary Reader*, 3rd ed., 554-575. New York City: NYU Press.

How I Show Up: Black and Excellent

Troy E. Boddy

"You have to be 10 times better" was the message our parents delivered to me and my siblings growing up. The message called us to be Black and excellent. Unfortunately, this Black excellence was not always acknowledged or appreciated in the white spaces of public school teaching and leadership.

I was one of the newest teachers at Malcolm Johns Elementary School in 1992. I received a psychology degree from one of the top historically Black colleges and universities (HBCUs) and a master's degree in elementary education from a university in New England. I was young, Black, educated, and a second-generation teacher. I was following in the footsteps of my father, who was a teacher and principal during segregation. I was grounded in my commitment to educating children of color because I grew up hearing stories of outstanding Black educators who had an unwavering dedication to providing Black students with an excellent education that prepared them for a world that did not see them as valuable.

My mother said those segregation-era Black educators would not move on with a concept until everyone understood it. She would also share how she hated using textbooks handed down from white schools. My aunt said going to segregated schools was like a big extended family because your teachers knew your family, lived in your community, and were invested in your success. One common denominator was that they all had a strong sense of self and a commitment to the social well-being of others. This background clarified my role as an educator in schools where most students' families were new to the country, having come here to seek the American Dream.

I understood the seriousness of my role in laying a foundation for my students to develop a strong sense of self, empathy, and social awareness. I was also aware that my credentials, which exceeded those of most of my colleagues, created a secret dialogue that accused me of being uppity. The team leader was a white woman with some experience who later became a great friend and supported me. She cared about the children and was an excellent teacher and mentor. In addition, a few seasoned Black teachers also showed me the ropes and affirmed my existence and experiences in the workplace.

My official welcome to the school came when a white teacher burst into my classroom with a water gun and squirted me with water while I was hanging a bulletin board. I looked at her with a helping of rage and wonder and said, "Excuse me!" She laughed and said, "I thought you were building services"—which, in my mind, didn't excuse her. This would not be the last time during my career when my identity seemed out of place for my white colleagues. I have always wondered: If these mostly well-intentioned white teachers saw me as the "other," how were they teaching our mostly immigrant and poor students? How were they helping students develop a strong sense of self and the belief that they could do anything like my parents did for me and their parents did for them? How were they challenging students to engage and master the content?

Hillary Clinton had shared what many believe was an ancient African proverb, "It takes a village to raise a child." I wondered if our village was on the same page regarding what it took to educate our diverse learners. I reflected on the village my parents and aunt experienced, which ensured that children had self-awareness and social awareness to navigate a system that didn't work in their favor. I found that our village muted these experiences and replaced them with a color- and culture-blind ideology with a dash of low expectations.

There was another first-grade teacher who viewed me as an idiot. Now, I recognize that I was green (a new teacher), but an idiot I was not. She would fill my mailbox or desk with student worksheets. The woman had a worksheet or handout for everything and a folder for every month of the school year in her file cabinet. I modeled my teaching after Ms. Robinson, my white third- and fifth-grade teacher. Ms. Robinson had made learning fun by allowing us to apply our learning through hands-on learning activities, so worksheets were not my go-to teacher move. I believe that learning should be fun and messy. Malcolm Johns Elementary was created as a multiage primary school (grades K-3); our students stayed in the same class for four years. Mrs. Worksheet would decorate her room with ready-made charts and cute borders that rarely reflected the Black and Latino students who actually attended our school.

We collaborated with school reform giants like James Comer on his School Development Program, which focused on improving the learning experiences of poor and minority students through collaboration and consensus building; and Howard Gardner on his multiple intelligences theory, which acknowledged that we all express our intelligence in various ways. My classroom was one of the ones Gardner visited to see his work in practice.

In my classroom, I created borders and charts that looked like my students. I also gave them ownership in deciding what we would hang on the walls and creating charts and diagrams to support their learning. In this way, I worked to ensure that my students saw themselves and gave them a sense of autonomy. In his SCARF Model (see figure 3.1), David Rock (2008) describes five domains that every person needs in order to minimize threats and maximize reward in collaborating with others. These five areas are status, certainty, autonomy, relatedness, and fairness. Rock argues that these domains should be in place to ensure better learning environments for adults to teach in. I believed that my students were important and thus carried high status in my classroom. They were funny, bright, and excited to learn, and they worked hard to master or exceed any given outcome. I gave them choices on how they wanted to learn a topic or how they would demonstrate their knowledge.

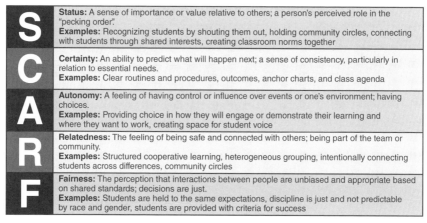

Figure 3.1   SCARF model.

Adapted from D. Rock, "SCARF: A Brain-Based Model for Collaborating With and Influencing Others," *Neuroleadership Journal*, 1 (2008); 1-9.

Meanwhile, across the hall in Mrs. Worksheet's room, the student experience was very different. While the teacher was caring, she had low expectations for our students. She would comment to colleagues that their parents didn't care about education and that she would hold back on teaching some concepts until the students were ready. She never really adopted the idea of multiple intelligences, beyond centers with ready-made worksheets for each of the intelligences, which she would make copies of for the teaching team. I would never use them, and one day she got so offended when she saw the reams of worksheets she had provided in my recycle bin that she confronted me about it and asked if I was too good for help. I replied that I believed that my students learned at deeper levels by being given opportunities to collaborate and apply their learning by doing engaging tasks that allowed them to problem-solve. I also reminded her that my students scored the highest on one of the county assessments in the fall, so I must be doing something right. I probably didn't need to add that last comment, but I knew it would push her buttons.

As my confidence grew during that first year of teaching, I began to interrupt what I secretly called the "White Girl Club." All the health teachers were white women, except for one other first-year male teacher who taught fourth grade. He was from a small town in Pennsylvania, and the only thing we had in common was our gender and the fact that we both liked beer. I was closest to the building service workers because we had much more in common; they took pride in my presence, and I took comfort in theirs.

I sat in meetings, situated with my Black male identity, and listened to the different ways in which some of my colleagues would talk about our majority of students of color. The comments ranged from what Lindsey et al. (2009) call **cultural destructiveness**, where the needs of a particular racial/cultural group are ignored, to **cultural proficiency**, where organizations respond effectively to the needs of diverse groups. Some of the comments were "They don't care about education," "These poor babies just need a safe place, and that is what we need to be for them," "They will not be ready to learn until they learn the language," and "Our kids will enjoy this unit; we just need to make sure they have the background knowledge to be able to make connections." Once I worked up the nerve to speak up, I interrupted some of these statements by asking questions like "How do you know?," "Do you know their families?," "Why would you think that?," "Did you know student X has his parents take him to the library every week?," and "What can we do to build background knowledge for our students?"

Counter-storytelling is one of the tenets of critical race theory. Counter-storytelling is the idea that the stories and lived experiences of Black people are valid data points. I learned that counter-storytelling was a valuable tool for interrupting talk that dismissed how our students and families experienced the world based on their limited exposure. Even I had to put my middle-class lens in check when I caught myself normalizing my background and invalidating theirs. My colleagues were often open to new perspectives, but in other cases, I would hear the standard "This is the way we have always done it." Over my 30-year career, I would learn that this was how white supremacy was maintained.

What struck me most about how our students and families were described was that this group of primarily white women felt they were the experts on this richly diverse community even though they had only a superficial knowledge that was too often based on hearsay. Some of them often spoke about our students and parents through a deficit lens, the same lens through which they looked at the community in which we taught. The only teacher that lived in the community was the other new African American female teacher; the rest of us did not live in the community we taught in.

Kleinrock (2021) suggests that educators must expand their lens from that of classroom teachers to that of community educators. This is how it was for the Black educators I was exposed to growing up, who taught during segregation and after. They were committed to the communities they taught in because they were part of those communities. Their asset-based lens allowed them to see the potential of the children they were charged to teach. My aunt, who attended segregated schools, said that the schools felt like family and that the children knew their teachers cared for them. In the back of my mind, I always had a running question: If the white teachers saw our Black and Brown students through a deficit lens, how did they see their colleagues of color?

At one of our weekly planning meetings, things came to a head. We were set to plan for an upcoming health education lesson on the definition of communicable diseases and how to prevent the spread of a communicable disease. Mrs. Worksheet came prepared with a folder of ready-made hand-outs she had collected over the years, but this time I arrived at the meeting armed with hands-on science experiments, videos, and other activities linked to the outcomes. My premise was that we would tell our students they were learning to be doctors, and as part of their learning, they would need to become skilled at diagnosing communicable diseases. I presented to the team the different ways we could engage the students using multiple intelligence theory. The culminating activity was to have students present for the community, sharing what they had learned. The team loved the information I presented—everyone except Mrs. Worksheet. She talked about students' behavior, whether it would be too much for them, and whether they even knew what doctors were. Her objections were overruled, and the team added to the ideas I shared.

Our students loved the activities, and our classrooms were abuzz with excitement. Some students even did extra research on the medical field based on what they were learning. During our debriefing, the team reflected on the unit, how engaged the students were, and the effort they put into their presentations. We read aloud several of the students' reflections on the unit and what they were proudest of. Many of the students reflected on how important they felt sharing their projects with the community. The majority of the students demonstrated mastery of the concepts. Our principal had observed several classrooms, including mine, during the unit and had written us a note praising our efforts to provide high-quality instruction and high expectations for our students. Mrs. Worksheet tried to pick apart the small things that could have been improved but eventually had to admit that the unit had been engaging for her students as well. She never acknowledged my contributions, but I never expected that from her. Knowing your worth is enough sometimes.

As the year progressed, the school principal came to me and said she had been contacted by UNICEF, which was looking for a classroom to shoot for an ad campaign. She let me know that she had selected my classroom. It was a great opportunity, and we would be part of a national ad campaign. When I shared the news with my team, many were excited that our school was selected, but Mrs. Worksheet looked at me and said, "She only picked you because you are a Black male." I just looked at her and thought that no matter how hard I worked and studied, the affirmative action mindset was a fixture in my chosen profession. But at the end of the day, I know my presence made a difference for thousands of students because I valued their experiences and was committed to their success.

Key Takeaways and Concluding Thoughts

People of color often have the role of being a member of a "minority" group and often can identify how racism plays out for students. They may have to "work 10 times as hard" just to get as far as their white colleagues. Living with these challenges can be exhausting because it adds a layer that other people do not have to consider. The perspectives and voices of educators who are Black, Indigenous, or people of color and other minorities are sometimes silenced or ignored, as described in Lisa Delpit's (1988) article "The Silenced Dialogue." This can happen when Black educators attempt to provide perspectives that challenge white supremacy culture. When heard, Black educators can add great value to addressing issues of inclusion and responsiveness. Educators of color must seek out peer groups and organizations where they can decompress and renew. White educators should examine the cultures they create and interrogate whether they are, in fact, inclusive of Black colleagues. This same interrogation of practices has to be carried out through educators' collectively building relationships with students so that Black students are not seen as a monolith but are instead understood to lead complex lives like all other groups of students. In this way, we begin to create inclusive learning spaces for the entire school community.

Discussion Questions

1. In what ways can educators ensure that students have autonomy and self-awareness in schools and classrooms?
2. *Differentiation* is a term that is used to describe how educators should make curriculum accessible to support diverse students, but school leaders often do a poor job of creating differentiated support for diverse educators. What lessons can be learned from the planning group and case study?
3. Who are the people who supported you early in your career? How do you support colleagues in navigating your school or district?

4. How might school leaders create spaces to support diverse staff?

5. How might feeling like the "other" cause diverse staff members to seek employment at other schools? How does being "othered" affect students?

6. What are ways you can create a more inclusive environment for your colleagues of color?

References and Suggested Resources

Brown, K.D. 2013. "Trouble on My Mind: Toward a Framework of Humanizing Critical Sociocultural Knowledge for Teaching and Teacher Education." *Race Ethnicity and Education* 16 (3): 316-338. https://doi.org/10.1080/13613324.2012.725039.

Castagno, A.E. 2014. *Educated in Whiteness: Good Intentions and Diversity in Schools.* Minneapolis, Minnesota: University of Minnesota Press.

Delpit, L. 1988. "The Silenced Dialogue: Power and Pedagogy in Educating Other People's Children." *Harvard Educational Review* 58 (3): 280-299. https://doi.org/10.17763/haer.58.3.c43481778r528qw4

Gateway Impact. n.d. "SCARF Classroom Environment Planning Tool—List of Strategies." Accessed December 18, 2022. https://gatewayimpact.org/sites/default/files/resource/files/SCARF%20Classroom%20Environment%20Planning%20Tool%20List.pdf.

Growe, R., and P. Montgomery. 2003. "Educational Equity in America: Is Education the Great Equalizer?" *Professional Educator* 25 (2): 23. https://files.eric.ed.gov/fulltext/EJ842412.pdf.

Kleinrock, L. 2021. *Start Here, Start Now: A Guide to Antibias and Antiracist Work in Your School Community.* Portsmouth, NH: Heinemann.

Lindsey, R.B., K. Nuri-Robins, and R.D. Terrell. 2009. *Cultural proficiency: A Manual for School Leaders.* 3rd. Thousand Oaks, CA: Corwin.

Mitchell, K. 2018. "Identifying White Mediocrity and Know-Your-Place Aggression: A Form of Self-Care." *African American Review* 51 (4): 253-262. https://doi.org/10.1353/afa.2018.0045.

Okun, T.O. 2021. "White Supremacy Culture—Still Here." https://drive.google.com/file/d/1XR_7M_9qa64zZ00_JyFVTAjmjVU-uSz8/view.

Ramasubramanian, S., E. Riewestahl, and S. Landmark. 2021. "The Trauma-Informed Equity-Minded Asset-Based Model (TEAM): The Six R's for Social Justice-Oriented Educators." *Journal of Media Literacy Education* 13 (2): 29-42. https://doi.org/10.23860/JMLE-2021-13-2-3.

Rock, D. 2008. "SCARF: A Brain-Based Model for Collaborating With and Influencing Others." *Neuroleadership Journal* 1:1-9.

Tatum, B.D. 2017. *"Why Are All the Black Kids Sitting Together in the Cafeteria?" And Other Conversations About Race.* New York City: Basic Books.

Whitehead, M.A., Z. Foste, A. Duran, T. Tevis, and N.L. Cabrera. 2021. "Disrupting the Big Lie: Higher Education and Whitelash in a Post/Colorblind Era." *Education Sciences* 11(9): 486. https://doi.org/10.3390/educsci11090486.

4

"Follow the Rules or Get Out of My Class"

Brendan Joseph Tassy

Future health educators must apply culturally relevant content to their lessons to develop a positive classroom climate that includes all students. A classroom climate that is respectful and inclusive of all students is one that is aware of and considers intersectionality. **Intersectionality** is the idea that people's interactions and experiences are created by the intersections of their individual experiences, such as race, gender, class, and sexual orientation. For example, a white, upper-class, heterosexual male will have a different experience than a Black, middle-class, lesbian female. To develop a classroom climate that is respectful and inclusive of all students, teachers need to be aware of the different intersections of their students' identities and be prepared to address any potential issues that may arise. As current and future educators, we must learn to accept ideas from others, cultural diversity, and diverse body types by engaging in cooperative and collaborative projects with our students through the mindset that all cultures and people have value in our classes.

Classroom climate refers to the learning environment and the culture of a classroom. As educators, we must focus on the climate over "managing" people. If we develop a place where all are valued and can be seen and heard, then "management" can be intuitive because intrinsic motivation is higher. The combination of many aspects, including instructional delivery elements (i.e., kinesthetic, auditory, visual, etc.), makes up a student's experience in a learning space. Classroom climate is important because it can affect a student's engagement, motivation, and overall learning experience.

A positive classroom climate can promote a sense of safety and comfort, regardless of gender, race, religion, sexual orientation, and any other personal qualities, which can lead to increased learning and academic success. It can also help develop positive relationships between students and teachers and create an atmosphere of trust and respect. Additionally, a positive classroom climate can help reduce stress and anxiety for both students and teachers, promoting better overall health and well-being. Especially now, with mental health and well-being being emphasized even more in education, it is important to do everything possible to make sure our students are healthy, not only physically but mentally and emotionally. Overall, classroom climate is an essential factor in creating an effective and successful learning environment for health education where students learn and practice health literacy skills across different real-life content topics.

Geographic Context for Case Study

Both Mr. Staple and Ms. Jordan are public school health educators at Allmass Regional Middle School (ARMS), which has a population of 937 students ranging from sixth to eighth grade. Located in an inner-city neighborhood, the school serves as a second home for many students in the area, due to issues at home. For a lot of the students, school is an escape from all the outside noise and drama they may be experiencing in their lives. Many of the students attending ARMS are students of color from a variety of backgrounds: different cultures, immigration statuses, and religions. ARMS has a very large Latino and South American student population. Many of the students who attend ARMS come from families who identify as lower middle class, choose to accept the school's free lunch program, and utilize the after-school program while parents or guardians work.

Overview of Teacher

Mr. Staple is a white, upper-middle-class, Catholic, heterosexual male. He is a very old-fashioned teacher who believes in strict rules and discipline and has very high expectations for his students. Mr. Staple has been teaching health education since 1990 and continues to practice with the same pedagogical methods he used when he started. Mr. Staple does not believe in autonomy: it's his way or the highway. Mr. Staple is a firm believer in traditional health education. He rarely gives students the freedom to explore their own ways of showing what they know in health education class, instead insisting that everyone follow the same routine with him: telling the students the content and applying it to a worksheet or scenario, or watching a video and answering questions. Mr. Staple also puts a strong emphasis on competition, often having students compete against each other in health-related games and challenges to win "prizes." He is quick to criticize students who do not perform to the standard he expects of them but rarely gives positive feedback to students. Students are forced to participate; otherwise, Mr. Staple threatens to fail them. His students always perform well on health tests, which is one of the reasons why he has been employed for so long. Overall, Mr. Staple is a strict, hostile, old-fashioned teacher who feels he doesn't get paid to build classroom culture. He is the teacher, so he is in charge of or has a position of power over his students. He believes his students come to his class ready to learn.

Ms. Jordan is a first-generation, middle-class, nonbinary, gay, African American health education teacher who has very strong interpersonal skills. Ms. Jordan uses she/they pronouns and encourages students to share their pronouns with her as well. Ms. Jordan has taught at ARMS for three years and has built strong relationships among the students. Ms. Jordan starts each class by giving students a few options for instant activities, encouraging them to work together to come up with the best ideas that will suit everyone's capabilities. Ms. Jordan's classes are far from boring. The students are encouraged to explore different fitness and health promotion activities, such as yoga, jogging, and online health education sessions. She also encourages them to step outside their comfort zones, for example by taking part in local mental health sessions or joining community fitness organizations. Ms. Jordan puts in her best effort to make health education class an enjoyable experience for all of her students. She wants to show them that health can be fun and doesn't have to be a chore. She also encourages her students to take responsibility for their own health and wellness by practicing health literacy skills, a lesson that will stay with them for years and promote lifelong learning and positive health. Ms. Jordan is a health education teacher who chooses to embrace autonomy and still provide an adequate education.

Mr. Staple's Health Class

When students arrive for Mr. Staple's class, they are expected to sit down immediately and aren't allowed to speak with classmates until they have submitted their completed instant activity. Desks are set up in rows facing the board. Mr. Staple does not greet the students when they arrive, and students do not look engaged or excited to be in the space. Currently, ARMS is in their nutrition unit, and Mr. Staple has decided to focus this class on his favorite part of nutrition, the food pyramid (even though it was updated by the United States Department of Agriculture [USDA] to MyPlate in 2011, he has not updated his teaching materials).

Once students have finished their instant activity and are ready to participate, Mr. Staple gets right to it. He first introduces nutrition to the class by having them all sit in front of him while he begins to briefly lecture, by reading off a PowerPoint he has been using for 20-plus years, on the history of nutrition from the USDA. The students show little to no interest in nutrition because the examples have no cultural significance to them. The food examples do not apply to many students in the class because Mr. Staple uses only Western diets for his examples. About 95 percent of Mr. Staple's class does not identify with Western culture because the students come from many different cultural backgrounds, such as South American and Caribbean. Since Mr. Staple's PowerPoint is very old, the figures and examples are outdated and do not relate to the majority of students in the class.

One student named Ria raises her hand and asks why none of the food in the PowerPoint looks like the food she and her family enjoy. "Mr. Staple, why doesn't any of the food look like the food I eat at home? I am really interested in learning about nutrition so I can stay healthy, but I don't see any plátanos, ensalada, or arroz con pollo." Mr. Staple does not know what any of those foods are, which causes him to feel embarrassed and insecure, so he snaps back at the student: "Ria, can you please stop interrupting class with your ridiculous food ideas? We are doing my type of nutrition because it is a traditional American diet, and we live in America." Ria's face begins to get red with embarrassment, not only because Mr. Staple has embarrassed her in front of the whole class but also because he has insulted her heritage and culture. She turns to talk to her classmate. When Mr. Staple sees this, he says, "You are now disrupting my class. Get out!" Ria is upset and doesn't understand; she was just trying to share her thoughts and then got kicked out of class.

After explaining the history, Mr. Staple begins to partner students up so they can design their idea of a nutritious meal. Mr. Staple likes to partner students who "look" the same. For example, he partners the Caucasian students with each other, the African American students with each other, and the Latino students with each other. He also makes sure to partner males with females. Sophia is partnered with a student named Alex. Alex is a Black, upper-middle-class student who identifies as a female and is in the process of transitioning from male to female. Alex has been looking forward to her middle school health education class all semester, especially the nutrition unit, because she loves to eat. Alex is partnered with another female student, which makes her feel uncomfortable. Being forced to partner up with someone of the same gender is something that Alex has dreaded from the moment she heard Mr. Staple starting to partner people up by gender. She feels her teacher doesn't have enough respect for her gender identity to pair her up with someone of the opposite gender, and he did not ask any of the students for their preferences. Alex wants to be seen for who she is, not what she is.

Alex feels awkward and out of place as she and Sophia begin the activity. She is afraid of being judged by her peers and feels like she is being put on display. When she voices her concern to Mr. Staple, he disregards it and says that her partner has nothing to do with her, that she should be focusing on nutrition and developing a healthy meal. She tries to focus on the steps Mr. Staple has recommended using to create a healthy meal and to ignore the stares she is getting, but it is difficult. At the end of class, Alex is relieved to be finished. The experience has been far more difficult than she expected, and it has taken a toll on her confidence. She is determined not to let it happen again, so she decides to start skipping health education class. Mr. Staple refuses to take responsibility for Alex's absences because he doesn't feel Alex should be partnered up with a boy while she is still a boy. Although he hasn't checked in with the other students, Mr. Staple worries that this would make them uncomfortable. Class ends, and Mr. Staple dismisses the students. It is now Ms. Jordan's turn to lead her health education lesson.

Ms. Jordan's Health Class

As students arrive, Ms. Jordan is projecting different types of food from the different cultures of the students that they had shared on their exit slips from the previous class. Before the nutrition unit started, Ms. Jordan gave every student a multiple-choice form, allowing them to select what types of food they enjoy so that she could use student voice to cater the nutrition to their cultures to make it more relatable. To start, Ms. Jordan highlights some of the history of traditional meals for each of her students' respective cultures and asks her students if any of them know anything about any of the meals she shows and why they may be healthy/nutrient dense or less healthy/lacking nutrients for a well-rounded diet. Manny raises his hand out of excitement as soon as the question leaves Ms. Jordan's mouth. Manny's parents regularly prepare one of the meals that Ms. Jordan showed during her presentation, so he explains his history with the meal and even shares with the whole class how his parents cook the meal, followed by resounding applause from his peers. Ms. Jordan then gives Manny a gold star, given out to students who participate in class and express themselves.

After Ms. Jordan goes over each of the steps to eating healthy, she begins to have students partner up. She switches the way she partners students with each other every day. Today she says, "I want you to partner up with a student who has the same color shoes as you." As students are finding partners, Ms. Jordan plays music specific to some of the cultures of the students in the background, and students begin to feel the rhythm as they find partners. Ms. Jordan notices a student who hasn't moved, so she approaches that student and asks why. The student's name is Rahul. Rahul is a slightly overweight East Indian boy who doesn't particularly like to talk about nutrition because it makes him feel fat. Ms. Jordan offers to play a song of Rahul's choice. He chooses a traditional Indian song, and immediately gets up and starts to move around. As the students begin to settle down with their partners, Ms. Jordan asks the class to show with their thumbs how they like the Indian music and Rahul's moves. The extremely positive responses make Ms. Jordan realize that she didn't include Indian cuisine as an option on the form she originally gave out.

At the conclusion of the lesson, Ms. Jordan asks the class how they enjoyed the lesson and promises the students that the next type of meal that they will talk about as a class is traditional Indian cuisine. Rahul's eyes light up, and he starts jumping for joy. He is extremely excited for the next lesson, and the other students began to get excited because they see how excited Rahul is. Although Rahul doesn't feel particularly comfortable talking about nutrition, the fact that Ms. Jordan is going to talk about Indian cuisine will help Rahul feel slightly more comfortable.

Ms. Jordan is a very thoughtful teacher, always reflecting on how she can make her classes better. As she stands in the empty classroom, she reflects about the success of the class, the enthusiasm of her students, and the overall experience. Ms. Jordan recognized that she missed an opportunity to highlight Rahul's culture and identified steps to build that into future classes. She is happy with the progress her students have made over the course of the semester. She is proud of the way they picked up the steps and learned the different cultures and how they eat. She is grateful for the support provided by her colleagues and the school administrators.

Key Takeaways and Concluding Thoughts

Having a positive classroom climate is important for student learning. Ms. Jordan's class's climate is much more positive than Mr. Staple's. Within Mr. Staple's class there are observable white cultural norms, including only one right way to respond, creating levels of competition, limiting views of others, and grouping strategies to further marginalize groups of people. On the other hand, Ms. Jordan attempts to collect student voices, shares multiple views and cultures, and is open to adapting future lessons. When she realized a student was "left out," she did not get upset but made adjustments to help that student feel included.

Collecting student voices and reflecting on the inclusion of all students will result in a better learning atmosphere, which in turn will promote better learning. It is crucial that students are focused and are comfortable in the classroom when learning a topic as important as health literacy skills and content because health education is a class that students can use immediately and forever. If students do not feel comfortable in the classroom, then they will be reluctant to be open to learning different perspectives. Having a bad association with health because of their experience in school can potentially harm them in the long term. Health education can also be a touchy subject for some, especially regarding hygiene, race and equity, and sexual health; so developing a classroom climate that supports embracing different perspectives, cultures, and ways of learning is that much more important.

At the end of the day, if your students are not comfortable in your classroom, they will not want to participate in, and in some cases even show up to, class. Health education is something that all students should have access to in order to learn how to take care of themselves and strive for lifelong health and well-being while avoiding and potentially preventing health-related diseases and illnesses.

The following are some suggestions for promoting a positive and comfortable classroom environment:

- Develop a classroom climate that encourages open communication and active listening.
- Create a safe and inclusive environment by addressing expectations at the beginning of the term and having students agree on them.
- Have students help decorate the classroom. This will make the classroom feel more welcoming and homey to them.
- Utilize feedback as much as possible, whether it be positive specific, positive general, or corrective specific feedback.
- Encourage students to take leadership and ownership roles, especially regarding their learning. This can be done by practicing autonomy in the classroom.
- Build relationships with the students as much as possible. Developing trust with them will help them open up if anything makes them feel uncomfortable. This in turn will help create a more supportive environment.
- Utilize different teaching methods because students have different learning styles, whether auditory or visual.
- Always ask for feedback from the students to gauge their understanding of the subject as well as to better understand the things that work well versus the things that can be modified.

Discussion Questions

1. What were the differences in classroom climate between Mr. Staple's and Ms. Jordan's classes? Consider white supremacy culture or white cultural norms in establishing classroom climate.

2. How did Mr. Staple's instructional delivery and classroom climate cause students to either be kicked out of his class or not want to go at all? What could you do differently to make your class climate uplift all types of intersectionality (socioeconomic status, race, ethnicity, religion, LGBTQ+, gender, body size, etc.)?

3. How may defining "American" culture belittle students and harm the classroom climate?

4. How does grouping students increase or decrease the valuing of marginalized groups? How can it further marginalize students in your classes?

Suggested Resources

Bhopal, K., and J. Preston, eds. 2012. *Intersectionality and "Race" in Education.* Vol. 64. Routledge.

Blitz, L.V., D. Yull, and M. Clauhs. 2020. "Bringing Sanctuary to School: Assessing School Climate as a Foundation for Culturally Responsive Trauma-Informed Approaches for Urban Schools." *Urban Education* 55 (1): 95-124.

Crenshaw, Kimberlé W. 2017. *On Intersectionality: Essential Writings.* New York: New Press. https://scholarship.law.columbia.edu/books/255.

Gillborn, D. 2015. "Intersectionality, Critical Race Theory, and the Primacy of Racism: Race, Class, Gender, and Disability in Education." *Qualitative Inquiry* 21 (3): 277-287.

Harris, A., and Z. Leonardo. 2018. "Intersectionality, Race-Gender Subordination, and Education. *Review of Research in Education* 42 (1): 1-27. https://doi.org/10.3102/0091732X18759071.

Khalifa, M. 2020. *Culturally Responsive School Leadership.* Cambridge, MA: Harvard Education Press.

Kieran, L., and C. Anderson. 2019. "Connecting Universal Design for Learning with Culturally Responsive Teaching." *Education and Urban Society* 51 (9): 1202-1216. https://doi.org/10.1177/00131245124518785012.

Black Joy

Deanna Toler Kuhney

They told us that we could not bring all of "these" Black girls together in the same space at the same time. They said, "You *will* need security present." Then they perused their list of potential participants and said, "These two can't be with those two." I sensed fear and immediately noticed my thinking changing. In the next breath, those same administrators talked about the goal of the intervention: to create an opportunity to inspire and empower the girls to "change the school, the community, and the world." In spite of the admirable goal, the joy I had felt anticipating the opportunity to work with Black girls had turned to trepidation. I had internalized their fear. I needed to self-correct.

Preparing Head and Heart for an Intervention

Research shows that formal schooling is often an inhospitable place for Black girls to learn in ways that bring their full humanities to bear because they are often compared to white femininity standards. Stereotypes held against them include being loud, overly sexual, too talkative, disruptive, and nonintellectual.

   I began to wonder, "How many of these presenting symptoms were really for the girls to own?"

According to *Stopping School Pushout for Girls of Color,* a report from the National Women's Law Center (Onyeko-Crawford, Patrick, and Chaudhry 2017), Black girls are 5.5 times more likely to be suspended than white girls and are more likely to receive multiple suspensions than any other gender or race of students. In Minnesota, Wisconsin, and Illinois, Black girls are 8.5 times more likely than white girls to be suspended. In the District of Columbia, where Black girls represent 73 percent of girls enrolled in school and 94 percent of all girls suspended, they are an astounding 17.8 times more likely to be suspended than white girls. This disproportionate discipline starts as early as preschool, with Black girls making up 20 percent of girls enrolled but 54 percent of girls suspended from preschool.

The request for me to support the intervention came shortly after the return to school amid COVID-19. The administration raised concerns about the number of Black girls who were not behaving positively with peers and not attending classes regularly. Some of the misbehavior was described as "drama." However, of greatest concern was the constant fighting among the girls.

As I listened, I wondered, "Do they notice white girl drama? Why are these girls skipping classes and why are they fighting? And has the administration investigated environmental factors as much as they have interrogated the behaviors of the girls?"

I came across an article in the *Washington Post* that expressed that COVID had incited a variety of social challenges for schooling, among them a notable rise in reports of in-school fights. Mo Canady, the executive director of the National Association of School Resource Officers, was quoted as saying, "School violence has risen to levels that we haven't seen quite frankly, and I don't think it took a genius to see this coming" (Meckler and Strauss 2021).

I wondered, "Did the school anticipate this mental health phenomenon, and what proactive measures were put in place to alleviate the fighting?"

The message I heard was that we needed to "fix" the girls to fix the fighting. The school administration's initial thinking for the intervention was to bring in speakers, as well as to use current academically successful Black girls to serve as mentors.

I wondered, "Who decides what success looks like, and who decides who decides? Would this approach be harmful in any way? Would the chosen mentors be respected and deemed loyal and trustworthy enough for our girls to receive from them?"

Zaretta Hammond (2014), in her book *Culturally Responsive Teaching and the Brain,* reminds us that if educators can establish one point of connection with our students, we can begin to establish a foundation of trust and relationship building which opens the door for learning and social-emotional well-being.

In my girlhood, our community code was loyalty and respect, which meant that you must have each other's backs. It was not written anywhere, but it was the culture. We lived the code in our behaviors. There were rewards for its presence and consequences in its absence.

I wondered, "Are the girls operating under a similar code, which influences the fighting?"

I grew up in a segregated-by-design (redlining), all-Black community. Our leaders and the majority of teachers looked like me until 1975, when we were bussed to a predominantly white neighborhood for junior high (known today as middle school). Our teachers became whiter, there were homes with driveways and white picket fences, and I heard talk of summer vacations that were very different from my own. Though I never heard anyone say that we didn't belong there, I sensed that we were "guests." The structures told me so. Everyone appeared to be polite, but our apparent differences made the Black students feel the need to be extra protective of one another. We (the Black students) were in the same building but not in shared space. During the school day, I believe, we longed for something familiar, so we stuck together whenever we could, especially during lunch and physical education.

I wondered, "How different was my experience from that of the Black girls today?

What does the author mean by the statement "We (the Black students) were in the same building but not in shared space"?

The most joyous part of the school day for us was gathering at the bus stop for our long ride home. Even in a sea of yellow buses, it was not difficult to find ours. If you didn't remember your bus number, you just looked for the bus with the students who looked like you, and you would get back to your neighborhood or close enough to walk. Our rides home were filled with laughter, jokes, and stories about our experiences that day. I often wondered if the white students, teachers, and parents in the school felt a measure of discomfort in their environment? Thankfully, for us, there was a measure of Black joy in the midst of our oppression.

What were the aspects of oppression and Black joy the author refers to by saying, "Thankfully, for us, there was a measure of Black joy in the midst of the oppression"?

Once at home, we rushed to change clothes and do our homework, so that we could gather at the centerpiece of our community—the basketball court. The girls jumped double Dutch, played jacks, or watched as the boys played their style of basketball, pushing and shoving to hold one another at bay. They called it defense. At times, it would become intense, and often quickly turn to joyful laughter. There were times of conflicts for sure, mostly due to a feeling of disrespect. The ugliest fights were because someone responded to a slight with "Your mama!" Upon hearing that, everyone would freeze and wait for the fight to begin. Those two words could spark a war. Being two-faced (smiling in someone's face and then talking about them behind their back) and being disloyal to our community ranked second and third in the way of offenses. We could talk about each other, but no other community could. There were definitely territorial boundaries, and there were fights within and among communities.

Our community code/culture had practices and structures, even for fighting. Both sides gathered on the field at the appointed time and formed a circle, and the two fighters (only two were allowed to fight at a time) entered the center of the circle. Those of us on the outside were there to serve as referees, ensuring that others did not jump in, making sure only hands were used to fight, and deciding when to end the fight. If a fighter was down too long or getting beat too badly, the fight was called. The rules were the same for both boys and girls, except boys were never allowed to fight girls. Ever. There were consequences for that.

I wondered, "How are our girls' cultures being perceived in their school space?"

Too often, the public discourse around Black people is focused only on pain, trauma, and the fight for freedom. It has centered oppression and suffering in portrayals of Black people and communities, while neglecting the beauty of our varied lives, cultures, and traditions, and the happiness that thrives within them. Just as there is no monolithic Black experience, there is no one definition of what Black joy is and what it feels like. The concept of Black joy debunks the narrative that Black people are unable to experience joy in the face of oppression by spotlighting the things that make life joyful.

To us, there was nothing scary about our community. Our jump rope rhymes were snappy and sassy, nothing worthy of "adultification." Our altercations were not out of control but very orderly. Our boys' style of defense was fair play, not an act of aggression punishable by suspension. At home, we could be ourselves completely. We created the rules and structures that supported our ways of being—our culture. We were able to define what was right and what was wrong. This was my Black joy.

Regrettably, I moved out of my Black community when I got married. Due to my husband's preference, we purchased a home in a predominantly white neighborhood and county. One day as I was walking my daughter to the bus stop, I asked her what she did during recess. She said they jumped rope. I was instantly reminded of the fond times I had jumping double Dutch on the basketball court. Curious, I asked, "Do all the girls know how to jump double Dutch?" I was wondering if white girls jumped double Dutch too. But my daughter gave me a strange look. Horrified, I exclaimed, "You don't know what double Dutch is? I'm your mother! How could this be?" Growing up, I don't recall anyone teaching me how to jump double Dutch—it was just something you did, like breathing. At that moment, I realized that my zip code, two-car garage, and manicured lawn had come with several additional costs.

While educational settings may be envisioned as safe spaces that facilitate learning, foster creativity, and promote healthy development for youth, research has found that this is not always true for Black girls. Their negative experiences within educational settings are both gendered and racialized, often communicating broader societal perceptions of Black girls that ultimately shape their identity development (Burnett et al. 2022).

Throughout the years, my daughter's intelligence, abilities, and humanity have been called into question by white educators, parents, coaches, and even children who called themselves friends. Ironically, I was now raising my children in the kind of neighborhood that I was bussed to as a child. Yet while I now lived in the neighborhood, my children, like me, were still seen as guests.

Preparing to meet the Black girls for the first time made me nervous, partially due to the way they were described by administration and partially due to my own insecurity. Was I the right Black woman to support these girls? Did I talk like them? Did I live in the right neighborhood? Would they see me as credible—someone worthy of their respect, loyalty, and trust? Would I feel familiar? I suspected many of these things would be as important to them as they had been for me as a Black girl growing up. In spite of these uncertainties, we three facilitators were certain about three things:

Three Must-Haves

1. We wanted all the girls together, regardless of their previous interactions.
2. Security would not be present in our space.
3. As facilitators, we had to have the autonomy to determine which adults (educators and/or administrators) could engage in this space with the girls.

Meeting the Girls

> It is our job as educators to not just teach skills, but also to teach students to know, validate, and celebrate who they are.
>
> —Dr. Gholdy Muhammad, *Cultivating Genius*

What initially started as a two-day intervention quickly and necessarily became four rap sessions, including our culminating outing. On the first day, we facilitators strategically positioned ourselves throughout the room ready to receive the girls. We also nervously wondered, "Would they show?" Our anxiety levels lowered only a bit as they trickled in. A few came willingly, most reluctantly, and some escorted by security, which we quickly cut off at the door. One by one, we greeted each girl with a lively welcome and hug, sharing that we were so glad to see them. Some smiled, while others rolled their eyes, but we weren't deterred. We trusted that full-fledged smiles would come.

The faces of these 18 girls reflected a kaleidoscope of color, experiences, and personalities. They were beauty, truth, authenticity, sass, laughter, protectors, and expert detectors of all things fake in word or deed. As they entered the circle with their beauty still illuminating beneath the "masks" they wore, we were prepared to prove ourselves worthy of their time and space. Of course we had to prove ourselves, because so much in their school experiences had taught them not to trust.

Through the intensity of the dialogue, we knew that two sessions would not be enough. By the end of the first session, we were already overwhelmed by the experiences from both in and out of school that came pouring out of these young bodies. They were 14 to 17 years of age. At times, each of us facilitators struggled to keep our heads and hearts balanced enough to be useful to the girls. The amount of burden and trauma below the surface was so much to carry. Thankfully, we weren't all feeling weak at the same time. That's one of the benefits of and reasons for not approaching this type of work alone.

No doubt experiences outside of school sometimes had an impact on the way the girls showed up at school, but this can be true for anyone. However, we gathered from the girls that the way they behaved at school was more a result of how they were received at school. School was triggering—our greatest takeaway of the day. On top of that, we also learned from administrators present that day that many of these girls had good grades.

I wondered, "Wait! What? Why was this piece of information missing or forgotten in my initial discussion with administration?"

When we asked the girls, "Why don't you attend classes?" the recurring theme was "The teachers get on my nerves, they get in my face, they get smart with me, or they don't talk to me at all. They're disrespectful!"

Zaretta Hammond believes that a key part of being culturally responsive as a teacher is recognizing that you are a critical linchpin in helping students navigate both the content and the classroom community. Unfortunately, there is still a cultural and racial mismatch between majority white teachers and majority students of color in most public school classrooms. Too often, implicit bias leads teachers not to see the cultural and linguistic assets and skills diverse students use to navigate the content. Too often teachers see culturally diverse students' behaviors as problematic (even when a white student engages in the same behavior without any consequences). This is implicit bias in action. The remedy is to help teachers expand their ability to recognize different ways of making meaning and engaging socially.

We thought, and now we knew, that Black girl work isn't for the faint of heart, for sure! You had better come prepared to be authentic, show up as a learner, be willing to be vulnerable, and have thick skin because when you are in a relationship with Black girls, they will drop some knowledge on you. They will tell you the truth about themselves, you, and everyone else. It is critical, in the moment, not to battle over whose truth is truer. We honored them all. More than what they said, we were most happy to just have them engage and be present in the space with us. We quickly realized that we were receiving a gift. Our sessions were layered, light, intense, tearful, triggering, bonding, insightful, gratifying, and beautiful—often all at the same time. We fought to keep some from walking away, and some left for a moment and eventually returned. Sigh!

By the end of our sessions, the girls knew that we were in it with them—not to fix them, but rather to help them be aware of and better navigate the broken system of education. "What happens when we shift from using loud, bossy, or aggressive to using bold resistors, innovators, and leaders?" asks Monique Morris (2016), author of *Pushout: The Criminalization of Black Girls in Schools*.

Since the school environment was a trigger for the girls, we took them to an outdoor retreat center for our culminating activity. There we engaged in confidence course activities that required camaraderie and teamwork. What we observed that day was nothing like the girls who were described during my initial meeting with the administration. To the contrary, we witnessed their collective brilliance and laughter as they collaborated, coordinated, communicated, and coached one another (and us adults) with maturity, empathy, and grace. Yes, at times it was a little messy, with some push and pull to successfully navigate through the course.

> *"How would their teachers and administrators perceive their push and pull? How would you?" "Messy or beautiful?"*

> *"Why are there patterns of Black girls only being perceived in one way—in a deficit way?"*

> *"Where does this culture come from, and would an examination of white supremacy culture provide some insights and opportunities for correction?"*

As facilitators we may not have resolved all or most of the administration's concerns, but they did acknowledge that we had engaged the girls in ways that they had not. I believe this success was based on our perspective that messy and beautiful can and must coexist in order to reverse deficit mindsets and to allow space for Black girls to create, embrace, and experience the joy they deserve.

Key Takeaways and Concluding Thoughts

Of course students, even Black girls, need to be accountable for their reactions and to understand how to navigate broken systems. However, adults must realize that child/student behaviors are generally symptoms, not the cause. Therefore, the following questions are offered to support educators and administrators in reflecting on policies, practices, and beliefs that harm academic and social-emotional well-being for Black girls in school spaces. Too often, there is a propensity to focus on elements that are outside of the school's control. The challenge is to focus inward.

Discussion Questions

1. What reactions are you experiencing as a result of this reading? What questions, connections, or challenges do you have?

2. How is health literacy skill development questioned and embraced? Consider analyzing influences, self-management, advocacy, and interpersonal communication.

3. What is the significance of the Three Must-Haves defined in this story?

4. What are some examples of ways students of color could be made to feel like guests in your school?

5. What does centering Black girls mean to you? How are Black girls centered in your classroom and school? What are some examples of changes you can make to your practices and policies to center Black girls? How will you measure the success of change?

6. What did the facilitators do throughout this experience to foster trust and build relationships with and among the girls?

7. Which characteristics of white supremacy culture most hinder your relationships and incite deficit narratives about Black girls in your school space?

8. How will you begin to counter deficit narratives about Black girls in your spaces? What skills and abilities might you need to acquire to better support Black girls?

References and Suggested Resources

Burnett, M., M. McBride, M. Green, and S. Cooper. 2022. "'When I Think of Black Girls, I Think of Opportunities': Black Girls' Identity Development and the Protective Role of Parental Socialization in Educational Settings." *Frontiers in Psychology* 13. www.ncbi.nlm.nih.gov/pmc/articles/PMC9358241/pdf/fpsyg-13-933476.pdf.

Ferlazzo, L. 2015. "'Culturally Responsive Teaching': An Interview With Zaretta Hammond." *EducationWeek*, July 8, 2015. www.edweek.org/teaching-learning/opinion-culturally-responsive-teaching-an-interview-with-zaretta-hammond/2015/07.

Hammond, Z. 2014. *Culturally Responsive Teaching and the Brain: Promoting Authentic Engagement and Rigor Among Culturally and Linguistically Diverse Students.* Newbury Park: Corwin.

Meckler, L. and V. Strauss. 2021. "Back to School Has Brought Guns, Fighting and Acting Out." *Washington Post*, October 26, 2021. www.washingtonpost.com/education/2021/10/26/schools-violence-teachers-guns-fights/.

Mohammed, S. 2022. "UK Black History Month: What Does Black Joy Mean to You?" Soho House (website), October 1, 2022. www.sohohouse.com/en-us/house-notes/issue-006/work/what-does-black-joy-mean-to-you.

Morris, M.W. 2016. *Pushout: The Criminalization of Black Girls in Schools.* New York: New Press.

Muhammad, G. 2020. *Cultivating Genius: An Equity Framework for Culturally and Historically Responsive Literacy.* With a foreword by B.L. Love. New York: Scholastic.

Okun, T. 1999. "White Supremacy Culture." dRworksbook. www.dismantlingracism.org/uploads/4/3/5/7/43579015/okun_-_white_sup_culture.pdf.

Onyeko-Crawford, A., K. Patrick, N. Chaudhry. 2017. *Let Her Learn: Stopping School Pushout for Girls of Color.* Washington, DC: National Women's Law Center. https://nwlc.org/wp-content/uploads/2017/04/final_nwlc_Gates_GirlsofColor.pdf.

Sadovi, C. 2022. "UIC Professor Honored for Teaching How to Search for Joy in Classroom Lessons." *UIC Today*, January 10, 2022. https://blackresources.uic.edu/news-stories/uic-professor-honored-for-teaching-how-to-search-for-joy-in-classroom-lessons/.

6

Learning From Landi

Porsche Vanderhorst

In a professional development module entitled "Black and Brown Girls: Building Understanding to Promote Engagement," facilitators take time to frame the learning experience with these three points:

1. *There is nothing innately wrong with our Black and Brown girls.* The dominant culture has been centered in United States public education. In the United States, the dominant culture is that of white, middle-class, Protestant people of northern European descent. (This term, *dominant culture*, is not used to affirm dominance but rather to reference cultures that assert or attribute dominance, usually through and resulting in the marginalization of others).

2. *There is nothing innately wrong with our Black and Brown girls.* United States public education was not conceptualized nor is it being reconceptualized with Black and Brown girls in mind. It was conceptualized for those who were a part of the dominant culture.

3. *There is nothing innately wrong with our Black and Brown girls.* Professional learning and development experiences for educators are often conceptualized based on the norms of the dominant culture and to the benefit of students of the dominant culture. Educators often miss out on professional growth opportunities that center non-dominance-asserting cultures.

The repetition of *"There is nothing innately wrong with our Black and Brown girls"* was quintessential to ensuring that the module participants knew they were not about to learn what can be done *with* Black and Brown girls. Instead, they were there to learn what can be done *for* Black and Brown girls, in affirmation and in honor of who they are, who their people are, and all they bring to the educational space. Stating the obvious, though often unspoken, truth that public education and educational professional development are rarely created specifically to benefit Black and Brown girls was necessary to ground participants' engagement with and commitment to the fact that the learning experience had one intended outcome: for Black and Brown girls to directly reap the benefits of what participants learned in the module. In the same way, this case study is intended to ultimately benefit the Black and Brown girls who grace its readers' health and physical education spaces of learning.

In *Black and Brown Girls Matter: Pushed Out, Overpoliced and Underprotected*, Dr. Monique Morris (Williams et al. 2015) admonishes readers to "develop the public will to address the challenges facing Black and Brown girls and other girls of color through elevating their experiences and engaging stakeholders to become actively involved in their welfare." This case study will undertake Dr. Morris' charge by examining an interview with Landi, a 16-year-old 12th grader of Afro-Latina heritage who attends public school. Landi took several high school classes while in middle school, positioning her for early graduation. Landi looks forward to graduating and attending a historically Black college or university (HBCU) close to home. Her mother is immensely proud of her daughter's academic accomplishments and excited that she will be staying close to home. Landi's interview takes readers through her experience of taking health and physical education courses in her school while at the same time being a part of a community step team. Landi's story provides direction for health and physical educators committed to creating spaces that specifically benefit Black and Brown girls.

What physical education classes did you take, and how did you feel about them?

Ok, so, I have participated in dance classes versus taking actual PE. I would say that the dance classes would be, for me, considered more physical than actual PE because—I don't know if it is more to show how they regulate the class—but with dance, we're constantly doing something every day, and it's exploring different genres of dance throughout the entire semester. And we actually had two shows during the semester, and I actually enjoy doing that.

Ok, so you are working toward something.

Yes.

Did you take health education classes as well?

I'm currently taking health this semester, actually.

Tell me about that.

So far, um, we have learned about drug misuse and use, mental illnesses, things like that. I wouldn't say that the class is necessarily educational. I feel like the things that are taught are self-explanatory or things that you grow up learning per se.

What do you feel is missing that would make it educational?

That's a good question. I think what's missing is applying it to realistic situations.

Tell me about your experience. When you think about being in dance class as an Afro-Latina, tell me about dance class through that lens.

Well, through that lens I would say that although we are learning different genres, we're not necessarily learning diversity throughout the genres. I would say that a lot of the things I'm taught do not have any cultural background as far as for people of color or people of different ethnicities. There's no teaching about that.

What are there teachings about?

Ballet, jazz, modern. It's mainly those three. If we do some hip-hop, we don't really get any education behind it. The teacher may make up some choreo, but that's about it. And we're also limited. When we do the semester showcases, we are limited to what we are able to do. And that's another thing that would … Let me not go ramble on. I don't want to go too far.

You're not rambling at all!

So the thing is, we're very limited as to what we're allowed to showcase. One of the problems I've noticed in our school is that a lot of dances of African descent or of Black culture are [looked at as derogatory]; and a lot of the teachers or the principal may even say that you know it's inappropriate or they don't agree with it, see. So we are not fully able to express our creativity through the dance. They think it's too sexual or something. Even though they didn't exactly say that.

How does that affect your heart, or your mind, or your spirit?

It makes me feel as though I have to reach out through different outlets in order to enjoy what I actually like to do, which is why I joined teams outside of school. Because I actually even tried to start a majorette dance and modeling team!

Wow! We were going to have some J-Settes in the public school? [*Note:* "J-Setting" is a subset of majorette dancing. It was developed at Jackson State University in the early 1970s and adopted by HBCUs' majorettes and dance lines.]

Yes! And I made it happen—however it was definitely a hassle in making it happen.

So, I hear your experience in your dance class. I want you to talk to me about your experience with the step team. How do you experience that as an Afro-Latina?

Okay, well for starters, I began step in middle school. It was a step team that was based in school, and I loved it. That's where I originally found my passion for stepping. Growing out of middle school and coming into high school, it was very hard for me to find teams, and I was in a position where I was like, I need to get into something in activity after school. And somebody's younger sister at my school introduced me to the team; and the first day I just came to one of their practices, and I immediately fell in love.

What pulled you in from day one?

They welcomed me—from the coach to any of the parents sitting there at the practice, even the girls—they automatically just threw me in there. They said, "Hey, learn some steps," and I said, "Okay. I'm a little rusty, but I'm going to do it!"

So after that first practice, you knew you were going to want to go back?

Definitely, and I knew that it was something that I wanted to fully commit to. It also felt like a challenge to me as well, with being a travel and competitive team— you get a whole different perspective of the step world. With certain schools, you only attended one competition per year, but we never actually learned about step. I feel like with this team we are learning what goes into step, more so than [just] technically the background, history—everything that just goes into a how step incorporates theater, dance, singing. There's more than just step: there's a whole bunch of performing arts that make your routine well rounded.

You are giving me life! I just need you to know that right now.

Thank you.

So I hear a contrast between how you experience dance class—although you do enjoy dance in general—but I hear a difference in the way you're talking about these two spaces of physical and performance engagement. Is there explicit teaching on the step team connected to culture, or is it just natural in what you're doing? Tell me about that.

I would say it's a mixture of both. Not only does it come from the demeanor of the coaches, but Coach N. and Coach S. make sure that every single one of us on that team understand who we are as young Black women, and [they] make sure that we understand that in this society we have to push harder than everyone else as a minority. And you know Coach does not play about grades at all, so she makes sure she incorporates that too. She tells us that grades come first, and some of the girls have to come into practice and study or do whatever, and if they need help with math or writing, all of us are there for each other in multiple aspects.

Do you think that could be possible within your school dance experience?

No.

Tell me why.

Because the drive, the drive is not there. Most of the people who do take the class, they're taking it because they need the credit for graduation. They're not necessarily taking it because "Oh yeah, I want to create this bond with everyone here." And it also falls back on the teacher. The teachers don't show that they care either. The teachers want you to show up, do what they tell you to do, and that's that.

Thinking about the health education part, how does step help with health education?

Well, okay—so me, naturally I've always been on the heavier side, and as soon as I started step I [felt] more confident about my body quickly, and this was without even me trying. I wasn't even deliberately trying to lose weight and lost a few pounds … because our practices are almost like HIIT workouts. When we step, we're stepping full out throughout pretty much the entire practice, and that's two and a half hours, two days a week, sometimes three, maybe four if there's a competition. So we're constantly active, but not only that, we're also doing conditioning. We're actually doing exercises that help us be stronger because what people don't realize is that with step you're forcing your body to do a lot of hard movements and you're contracting your muscles, you need to be precise, so you can't be floppy. You can't be wiggly all over the place. Your muscles have to be tight. The body has to be real straightforward, and all of that just takes so much energy from your body that you wouldn't even realize.

So that health part is built in without a doubt through physical well-being.

Most definitely. It also helped me be conscious of my health as well because I know for myself breathing has been an issue for me. And we're doing complicated routines—that's something that I think to myself, "Okay, I want to get myself better and in shape so that I can properly execute these routines." So with also doing the actual physical part it allows you to think or reflect upon yourself and your own health, and it shows you at what point you're in with your health. I also like that it gives me a group to hang with, help me with school, and expect more from me.

What is it that you as an Afro-Latina or person of Black African descent would want from your in-school health education experience?

I would want for the teachers and staff in general to educate themselves enough to be able to properly educate the students that are sitting in their classes for everybody. Not necessarily a book that is given to them or off the simple criteria that they have to follow or just one "right" way: "Don't have sex, say no to drugs, don't do this…" We are going to try things we shouldn't. We are kids. Give us more on what we can do when we don't want to do something or feel uncomfortable or a teacher is treating us different. More so, take that extra step further to properly educate every single person in that classroom so that everyone can feel not only heard but also seen in a sense.

You have given me a framework and a foundation that I think—no, I *know*—will make a difference for these teachers and leaders who are going to read this book and this chapter. So thank you, thank you, thank you. You're getting ready to change some other students' experience just from what you're saying now.

I'm glad I can participate and help.

Key Takeaways and Concluding Thoughts

Long before Black and Brown girls step into their school health and physical education classes, they are engaging in education on health, well-being, and movement via their ancestry, their homes, and their communities: shopping, preparing, and eating nutrient-rich traditional foods, attending and participating in movement-filled celebrations and sacred services, reaching out to community healers, being mentored by community coaches, taking family walks, watching from the cradle as Abuela dances, and charting plays from the stands as Baba coaches. All around and in them are deep roots of health and physical well-being. However, those roots are often left unnurtured when they enter formal physical and health education spaces in schools because a single narrative of what is supposed to be (a dominant white narrative) is presented. This includes communication, practices, sports, activities, body types, food, and so much more. These spaces are supposed to help them grow in the understanding and practice of wellness; and while Black and Brown girls can and do excel in these spaces in great numbers, many are left undernourished at best and completely disengaged or offended at worst.

If you are able, read these next three sentences aloud.

Black and Brown girls are led through a health and physical education curriculum that was not created with them in mind. Black and Brown girls are led through a curriculum that was not created with them in mind. Black and Brown girls are led through a curriculum that was not created with them in mind.

It is not untrue that Black and Brown girls are led through a curriculum created with white girls and white boys in mind, even if only subconsciously. This is a truth that educators must grapple with and settle in themselves if they are committed to the work of justice in education. And it shouldn't take too much to convince you—just conduct a Google search of the people or institutions that develop the curriculum and standards, and you will see that they are not people or institutions who have explicitly committed themselves to the excelling of Black and Brown girls in physical and health education (and no, saying "All students benefit" does not count). And if that doesn't convince you, take the word of Landi, who minced no words sharing that her community step team nourished her physical and mental health in ways that her classroom experience did not.

Landi's community step team was a space that was planned with Black and Brown girls in mind. Both her coaches and teammates contributed to that with intention. Landi was well aware of the intention in her community step team and the lack thereof in her physical education class. Recall that she said her physical education class "[does] not have any cultural background as far as for people of color or people of different ethnicities. There's no teaching about that." And when asked, "What is it that you as an Afro-Latina or person of Black African descent would want from in your school health education experience?" Landi replied, "I would want for the teachers and staff in general to educate themselves enough to be able to properly educate the students that are sitting in their classes for everybody. Not necessarily a book that is given to them or off the simple criteria that they have to follow. … More so, take that extra step further to properly educate every single person in that classroom so that everyone can feel not only heard but also seen in a sense."

Educator, author, and brain researcher Zaretta Hammond, in a 2016 webinar entitled "Tips for Culturally Responsive Lesson Planning," shared the practice of mapping cultural reference points. Figure 6.1 is an expansion on this process that could help you do as Landi wisely advised.

In light of this case study, here are some possible questions that could be asked of the Black and Brown girls in your health and physical education spaces for step 2 in figure 6.1.

- What does movement mean to you?
- What do health and well-being mean to you?
- What did movement mean to your ancestors/culture/country?
- What did health and well-being mean to your ancestors/culture/country?
- What kind of movement do you enjoy most? Why?
- What components of wellness do you enjoy most? Why?
- What sports do people play at family events?

Elevating Culture for Curricular Connection

1. ***Think about yourself*** and what you are about to do.
   - How do I feel about asking my students for cultural reference points?
   - How do I feel about planning lessons with specific student groups in mind?
   - If I feel nervous, unsure, or reluctant, who will I connect with to process these feelings and overcome them for the honor and benefit of students and the honor and elevation of my practice?
   - If I feel excited and hopeful, what is the source of these feelings, and are they student centered? Who will I connect with to process these feelings and share my plans for support and accountability?

2. ***Collect cultural information*** from students and compile it so that you can access it easily. Possible information to collect can include but is not limited to the following:
   - What they are watching
   - What they are listening to (music/podcasts)
   - What they enjoy eating
   - Social media accounts they recommend you follow
   - Causes that are important to them
   - Traditions they have and special days they observe
   - What makes them happy or proud
   - What is going on in society or globally that bothers them
   - Sayings or quotes that they or their families live by
   - People who are meaningful to them (present-day heroes, historical figures, ancestors, neighbors, family members, etc.)

3. ***Research the info*** the students give you, especially if you don't know what it is! This is a *must*. You don't have to become an expert, but you must be knowledgeable enough to use the cultural reference point wisely and respectfully.

4. ***Plan your lessons*** with the cultural reference points in front of you.
   - Match the reference points to the skill/concept you are planning to instruct.
   - Plan how you will embed the cultural reference point(s) into the lesson.
   - Have in mind who you want to be affected in that specific lesson (more engaged, alert, showing enjoyment, participating, etc.) by the use of the selected cultural reference point(s).

5. ***Teach and observe the lesson***, noting the impact of using the cultural reference point(s).
6. ***Reflect on the impact*** on students.
   - After teaching the lesson, how do I feel about my choice of cultural reference point(s)?
   - How did the learning experience pan out? Did I see the impact I was hoping for?
   - How did those specific students I had in mind respond? How did other students respond?
7. ***Reflect on the impact*** on yourself.
   - What was it like for me to plan to use cultural reference point(s)?
   - What was it like to implement the learning experience?
   - What did I learn about myself?

Figure 6.1   Process of evaluating culture for curricular connection.

Adapted from Z. Hammong, *Adapted Tips for Culturally Responsive Lesson Planning,* (2016). Adapted by Porsche S. Vanderhorst, LLC (2022).

- What wellness activities does your family engage in most?
- What dances seem to get everybody up no matter the skill level?
- What dances are social, and are there dances that are sacred?
- What tips do the elders in your community give for staying healthy?
- What home remedies does your family use when someone gets sick?
- Who is your family healer?
- Who in your life do you consider a role model for health? Why?

I hope you consider using this process. If you do, I do not advise you to do so in isolation. Seek support and accountability. Partner with a colleague, plan with your team, seek the support of a mentor, or reach out to me. Even consider letting the students know what you are working toward in your growth as a teacher ("I know the content I teach is important, but even more important to me is that you connect to the content. That's when learning happens best, and you deserve to learn the best way possible") and seeing what input they have. Perhaps there are volunteers who'd like to help you select some reference points that you will explore as you plan. Many students love to contribute to what they learn and how they learn it. You might even inspire future teachers when they see how you are approaching the craft.

But beyond the process, I hope that you learn from Landi and that her words inspire you to reenvision your health and physical education spaces in ways that directly benefit the Black and Brown girls you serve. I believe that you can and that you will.

Discussion Questions

1. What feelings and reflections did Landi's words stir up in you?
2. What do you think it would take for Landi to speak about her school experience the way she did about her community step team experience?
3. What would it take for your students to speak about their health and physical education experience the way Landi spoke about her community step team experience?
4. How does what Landi describes of her in-school experience sound similar to or different from the health/physical education spaces in which you serve?
5. How does what Landi describes of her experience with her community step team sound similar to or different from the health/physical education spaces in which you serve?
6. What can you do to reenvision your health and physical education spaces with Black and Brown girls in mind?
7. Are you knowledgeable about health, well-being, sports, and other movement-based traditions that may connect to the ancestry or home cultures of the Black and Brown girls you serve? For example, take a look at the terms listed below. Look them up and consider how they could be incorporated into viewing, learning, practicing, and making meaning connected to physical education standards.
   a. Capoeira
   b. Gumboot dance
   c. Kwepena
   d. Ngolo
   e. Rezball
   f. Stepping

References and Suggested Resources

Crawford-Garrett, K., D.R. Carbajal, A. Short, K. Simpson, E. Meyer, and E. Deck-Stevens. 2020. "Teaching Out Loud: Critical Literacy, Intergenerational Professional Development, and Educational Transformation in a Teacher Inquiry Community." *New Educator* 16 (4): 279-295.

Earick, M.E. 2009. *Racially Equitable Teaching: Beyond the Whiteness of Professional Development for Early Childhood Educators*. New York City: Peter Lang.

Hambacher, E., and K. Ginn. 2021. "Race-Visible Teacher Education: A Review of the Literature from 2002 to 2018." *Journal of Teacher Education* 72 (3): 329-341.

Hammond, Z. 2016. "Tips for Culturally Responsive Lesson Planning." https://drive.google.com/file/d/1zOjRfiAUiPA9wZ-yzKOGIqRxvyN39ZEK/view.

Leonard, A.M., and R.H. Woodland. 2022. "Anti-Racism Is Not an Initiative: How Professional Learning Communities May Advance Equity and Social-Emotional Learning in Schools." *Theory Into Practice* 61 (2): 212-223.

Salazar, M.d.C. 2018. "Interrogating Teacher Evaluation: Unveiling Whiteness as the Normative Center and Moving the Margins." *Journal of Teacher Education* 69 (5): 463-476.

Searle, K.A., C. Tofel-Grehl, A.M. Hawkman, M.I. Suárez, and B.L. MacDonald. 2022. "A Case Study of Whiteness at Work in an Elementary Classroom." *Cultural Studies of Science Education* 17 (3): 875-898.

Williams, K., C. With, P. Ocen, and J. Acknowledgments. 2015. *Black Girls Matter: Pushed Out, Overpoliced and Underprotected*. New York City: African American Policy Forum/Center for Intersectionality and Social Policy Studies. www.atlanticphilanthropies.org/wp-content/uploads/2015/09/BlackGirlsMatter_Report.pdf.

7

The Danger of a Single Narrative

Daryl C. Howard

Hueville is a large suburban school district with a solid reputation and academic profile. The district receives high praise for being progressive, but there is always room for growth. The school system has representative diversity among student demographic groups, but the data suggests that students of color are disproportionately underperforming in contrast to their white and Asian counterparts. Additionally, as with most school districts across the country, although the student population is diverse, many of the teachers are women, and most of them are white. The teachers in the district are known as a mix of those who deeply care for their students and those who feel that certain students and families don't value their education.

"Dr. Brown, I need to speak with you," said Ms. White. "Sure! Your favorite high school counselor is always available to talk to his favorite teacher. What's up?" said Dr. Brown with a smile. "Dr. Brown, I just saw my roster for this year, and there are three students I am concerned about from our feeder middle school. They are on my class list, and I'm not sure they are the type of students who should be in my class," said Ms. White. Dr. Brown replied, "Well, tell me more. What's the issue? Why are they a concern for you?" Ms. White responded briefly, "I have to head to a meeting. Just take a look at the articulation notes from the previous school."

As the school counselor, Dr. Brown wasn't surprised by a teacher looking at their roster and wanting to make changes. However, Ms. White was a long-standing colleague and a solid teacher, so the angst over these students was concerning. Dr. Brown pulled out the notes from the middle school teachers and proceeded to read up on the three students. He saw that the three students had a few similarities: They were African American or Latino, they were boys, and they were all on free or reduced lunch. Additionally, not one single note in the articulation minutes indicated that any of the students were positive contributors in any way to their learning environments. With that introduction, Dr. Brown knew he had to prepare for these students who were coming to the high school.

As Dr. Brown sat in his office and reflected on what he had just read, there was ping from his computer. It was an email from a different teacher requesting a time to meet with Dr. Brown to discuss some schedule concerns. The message was about students possibly not having background knowledge for the subject, not being able to handle the rigor, or not having access to appropriate support. In short, it was riddled with low expectations and negative assumptions. Before responding, Dr. Brown checked the teacher's roster and found his suspicion confirmed: the three students Ms. White had flagged were on this teacher's caseload as well. Dr. Brown could feel a clear narrative building, so in response, he asked the teacher to share the names of the students so he could research them and learn more; he and the teacher would then find a time to talk.

Dr. Brown leaned back in his chair and pondered his next steps. To be proactive, he sent a message to all of his team teachers that if they had trouble with any students this year they should send the students to him instead of to the vice principal's office. "I want a chance to meet the students first," he typed in his message.

By the time the students showed up on the first day of school, Dr. Brown had decided his approach would center on intentional interactions and getting to know all of his new students. Unfortunately, it didn't take long for one of the three students to be sent down to his office. When the student arrived, he knew the relationship building would begin. Dr. Brown thought to himself, "This lanky kid is one of the students causing concerns? Am I missing something?"

Tyrell, an African American male with a tall, slender build, came in angry that the teacher had asked him to leave class. The note had little detail, stating only that the student refused to cooperate and engage. Dr. Brown was super busy scheduling new students, but he knew he had to stop and meet with Tyrell right then; he didn't want to send him a dismissive message. Dr. Brown said, "Come on in, young man! Have a seat, let's chat." Tyrell began defending himself: "This teacher isn't fair, she—"

"Hold up," Dr. Brown interrupted. "Let's not talk about your teacher. I'm going to be your counselor this year, so tell me about who you are."

Dr. Brown threw a small fidget ball at Tyrell, who caught it. Dr. Brown said, "How was your summer?" Tyrell looked perplexed, but he answered. They tossed the ball back and forth while talking about things that were non-school-related, such as family, hobbies, and favorite video games and music. It was clear to Dr. Brown that Tyrell didn't have many opportunities to share who he was and let people get to know him.

Dr. Brown slipped in a question asking if he liked his teachers from the morning. Tyrell replied, "Of the four I met so far, only one was nice. The only class I've liked so far is health. I can't remember his name, but he seems like he is going to be a cool teacher." Dr. Brown asked, "Why do you say that?"

Tyrell said, "Well, first off, the class didn't feel like a quiet museum when I walked in. The teacher said 'what's up' to everyone as they walked in, and he played music. He gave us some rules—he called them norms or something like that—and he told us how the class would be set up. He gave us a syllabus for the class and also a QR code so we can access class stuff from our phones. I thought that was dope. From there he told us we could talk and explore the magazines and posters on the walls from former students and in the digital classroom. He told us to think of a project where we research something about our or a family member's health or something we are passionate about to advocate for to make a change in our community. During this time, he called different students over to his desk and asked for one strength, one favorite song, and one interesting question about wellness or well-being. He wrote it down on a clipboard. Oh, I almost forgot, he had on the new multicolored Vans sneakers! Pretty cool for a teacher."

Dr. Brown chuckled and said, "Yeah, Vans are some of my favorite sneakers too." Tyrell looked at him, not sure whether to believe him or not. Dr. Brown asked Tyrell to tell him about the other teachers. Tyrell said, "They were boring, and they all seemed angry with me, and I didn't even do anything!" Dr. Brown thought back to the articulation notes from middle school and considered some of the messages Tyrell's high school teachers may have taken away from them. Dr. Brown said, "Sometimes teachers may be mean, and sometimes you may just think they're mean. Let's give it a chance and see where the truth lies."

He told Tyrell that ninth grade year was important and that he had to start off well no matter what. "You have to take responsibility for you." Dr. Brown said, "Over the next few days I want you to be observant of everything during your school day, and I'm going to call you back down later to hear your top five observations. Write it down." Dr. Brown wrote on a sticky note, "Pay Attention. Top Five" and gave it to him. Tyrell said, "Okay." He had clearly been in fight, flight, freeze, or fawn mode when he came in, but after some time with Dr. Brown he was able to reset and go to his next class.

Dr. Brown believed he had set the right tone with Tyrell and had likely begun to gain his trust. He jotted in his notes some of the key interaction points and what he thought the next action steps should be. He put a star on his calendar with Tyrell's name to mark when he would call him down to talk again.

On the second day of school, Marcus, a heavyset African American student, arrived to pick up his schedule. He was a day late because his mom hadn't submitted the proper paperwork for him to be enrolled, so he had been withdrawn from the system and couldn't start on the first day. As expected, there was no schedule yet for him when he came to the counseling office. When the secretary told him this, Marcus immediately pulled out his cell phone, called his mom, and told her he should just come home because his schedule wasn't ready yet. Dr. Brown overheard Marcus talking to his mom and told him he needed to speak with her.

On the phone, Dr. Brown introduced himself to Marcus's mom and asked how she was doing. He told her, "Ma'am, it's the beginning of the school year and I've had many schedule changes to do, but his schedule will be done shortly. There is no reason for Marcus to go home. He needs to be in class and learning." His mother said, "Thank you, Dr. Brown. He knows I can't pick him up at this time of day, but he was definitely going to try. I appreciate you giving me an update. Sometimes I don't want to talk to people at the school because they rarely have anything positive to say about Marcus. They say he is completely disengaged and insubordinate. That boy is going to send me to an early grave. Ever since his father and I divorced, I worry about him and wonder if he will make it out of school. All he wants to do is play video games and sports. My only wish is for him to be successful and graduate." Dr. Brown said, "I understand. I want the same for my children. High school will be a fresh start for Marcus. And guess what? I was just like him as a teenager. My mom and I laugh about it now. In short, I know it can be tough, but I have faith in his ability to have a great school year, and I will be calling and working with you to ensure that happens."

After Dr. Brown got off the phone, Marcus, who had heard the conversation, asked with a smirk, "Why'd you do that? You can schedule the other kids first and take your time with making my schedule." Dr. Brown replied, "Do you know what you want to do when you get older?" Marcus said, "Nope, and it sounds like you didn't either." Dr. Brown caught a sense of Marcus's wit and comebacks. He was a big guy, but Dr. Brown sensed he was a teddy bear under the exterior. Dr. Brown responded by saying, "You're right, and I definitely wouldn't have found out by sitting at home. I talked to your mother because I need you and her to know that I care about you and that your education is a big part of whatever dreams you have for the future. I also wanted your mom to know what I thought and that I will always call her with good and not so good updates. You are part of my community now, and it's my role to look out for you while you are here." Marcus just sighed and mumbled, "Bruh, why are you doing the most? No other teacher is doing all this extra stuff. What are you—a super teacher?" Dr. Brown smiled and said, "Yup, and we're going to be best friends by the time you graduate." Marcus looked up and couldn't help but smile.

Luis was the smallest of the three students, but he had the largest personality and the most to say about anything and everything. Everybody knew Luis. He was the small Latino kid with long hair who could always be seen in the cafeteria talking and being the center of attention. The second week of school, he nearly caused a school-wide fight in the hallways. It didn't really register for him until after the group mediation that being a small ninth grader and running your mouth in a large suburban school might not be a safe way to carry on. As a follow-up to the mediation, Luis and Dr. Brown were able to talk about the potential fight, what Luis had learned, and what things he could do in place of getting into other people's business. He was clearly shaken by the situation and anxious that it wasn't over. Dr. Brown sensed that this might be an opportunity for Luis to shift out of his current stage of development into something more industrious.

In their conversation, Dr. Brown asked a barrage of questions—he knew that Luis liked to talk and would be able to keep up with them. "How's your classes so far? Have you gotten to know your teachers yet? Do you feel you are off to a good start? Do you think your teachers like you?" Luis answered the last question first: "Some of them do. They tell me I frustrate them because I seem to have 'potential,'" he said, putting his fingers in air quotes. Luis continued, "Mostly my teachers tell me I'm smart but I waste my time getting involved in things that aren't productive." Dr. Brown asked, "Is that true?" Luis said, laughing, "Maybe. I typically finish my work quickly and then I get bored. Dr. Brown, I need things to do or I'm going to find ways to get into something. I have a lot of siblings, so I don't always get a lot of attention at home, so sometimes I overdo it at school. My parents tell me to stop being immature and make sure I get all my work done, so I do."

Dr. Brown told Luis that time is the one gift that all people are given equally and that how one uses it determines how successful they will be. He said, "It sounds like you are a bright kid, but maybe us educators haven't learned how to best meet your needs as an active learner. I'm going to talk with your teachers about some things that may keep your interest a little longer in class. In the meantime, I have an activity that I want you to complete." Dr. Brown gave Luis a blank chart with days of the week and times. He told Luis to fill in what he did seven days a week from the time he woke up to the time he went to bed. Dr. Brown also gave him a list of school clubs and activities that could potentially be good groups for him to join. Luis's assignment was to come back in two days with the schedule completed and be able to speak about what he learned about the clubs. Also, the assignment researching the various school clubs was to be in writing. Luis said, "Cool," and started to fill out the form. Dr. Brown said, "Hold up, you have to do the research first." Luis said, "Oh, my bad. I got you, Doc. I'll be back when I'm done," and walked out.

After having had a chance to meet with each of the students individually, Dr. Brown knew he had to think through how to remain a proactive and prosocial support for them. He began thinking about bringing them together collectively so that they could develop a schedule to routinely check in and create some opportunities for small-group reflection and discussion. As a counselor, Dr. Brown was very familiar with social-emotional learning, particularly how it looks through the lens of male students of color; this had been the thesis of his master's degree in counseling. However, a firm narrative about these boys had already been established—from their teachers, their parents, and maybe even the students themselves. They were seen as not serious about school, disruptive, and engaged in problematic activities. Dr. Brown decided to share updates with each of the students' teachers and to share the practices that the health education teacher used to foster relationships and set up a positive class climate, so they could incorporate the strategies into their classrooms. Part of his challenge would be to figure out how to help others see beyond the bias about these boys that might be lingering under the surface.

Key Takeaways and Concluding Thoughts

Building relationships is a common theme for many school improvement plans, especially upon returning to school after the global COVID-19 pandemic. Building relationships can be overwhelming for many educators, who see hundreds of students a day. The sense of urgency to get "through" content and other ideals of mainstream American culture creates barriers that can make teachers feel they don't have time to build these relationships. The weight of the written word from the previous schools identifying the Black and Brown males as problems created a barrier for the teachers to be open to receiving the students (whether this was conscious as with Ms. White or subconscious as with the other teachers).

How can you get to know every student? When you look at relationship building as an individual task, it is overwhelming because educators have many things to attend to on any given day. You can't do this work alone, but if you consider shifting your frame from seeing relationship as an individual endeavor to seeing it as the collective responsibility of every staff member in the building—at least starting with your team or department—then the task of relationship building is shared. While you may not have a deep relationship with a student, someone in the building does and can provide you with insight or partner with you to support students. Approaching this work through a collectivist lens better allows schools, departments, and teams to create inclusive environments that see students as more than a single story.

Discussion Questions

1. What were the moves and messages that the boys may have picked up from Dr. Brown?

2. Were any of Dr. Brown's approaches related to the social-emotional learning competencies (self-awareness, social awareness, self-management, relationship building, and decision-making)? Explain.

3. What did the health education teacher do that caught Tyrell's attention? What could help other teachers working with these students to recognize and leverage their cultural experiences, their stage of development, and how they learn as males?

4. What else would you recommend to Dr. Brown to help disrupt the bias and deficit-based mindsets that already existed about the boys?

5. How did the students' intersecting identities play out in this case? Consider race, size, and skin color.

Suggested Resources

The BOND Project (website). n.d. BOND Educators. https://bondeducators.org/.

Coalition of Schools Educating Boys of Color (website). n.d. https://coseboc.org/.

Hammond, Z., and Y. Jackson. 2015. *Culturally Responsive Teaching and the Brain: Promoting Authentic Engagement and Rigor Among Culturally and Linguistically Diverse Students*. Newbury Park: Corwin Press.

Maryland Public Schools. n.d. "Transforming the Culture Of Maryland's Schools For Black Boys." Accessed July 18, 2023. https://marylandpublicschools.org/stateboard/Documents/2021/0427/MSDETransformCultureforBlackBoy.pdf

8

"What's Your Pronoun?"

Tiffany Monique Quash

Jordan McIntosh was an average high school student who can be described as inquisitive and always challenging the world around them. Unlike other students, Jordan recognized early that they subscribed to neither the pronouns (*he/him*) nor the gendered clothes that were placed upon them from infancy based on the gender identified at birth (the external organs). Being Black and growing up in a household with two moms, Jordan was acutely aware that their family was different from heterosexual families. But Jordan knew their family was similar to heterosexual families because their lesbian parents loved and cared for them.

Jordan's parents, Cynthia and Madison, were accustomed to being welcomed in their queer-friendly community, unlike in other places they had lived. Cynthia and Madison had carefully chosen a community for their family, and they knew it was ideal because of the unwavering support they found as a couple and, when Jordan was born, as a family.

However, by the time Jordan reached the age of six, both parents began to notice that Jordan did not always enjoy wearing "boy" clothes and would often be found rummaging through their closets looking for clothes that would match how they felt on a given day. If none of these items could be found, Jordan would resort to making an outfit with accessories found throughout the house. Initially, Jordan only wanted to wear the outfits in front of their moms, but this soon changed into wanting to wear such clothing in school.

The teachers, the principal, and Jordan's moms supported what they viewed as Jordan coming into their "creativity" as a first grader, but this was not at all what happened. Everyone thought Jordan would phase out of wearing girls' clothes one day and would be wearing only boys' clothes by the end of the school year, but this never happened. In fact, Jordan's wearing of girls' clothes persisted throughout middle school.

By the first year of high school, Jordan's moms were able to find a community of other parents who had children who were beginning to change their pronouns and examine how they performed gender in society. The parents came from all walks of life, straight and queer, and from various races (except Black). The McIntoshes were used to being the only Black queer family, but at least they had a second community in which to discuss the importance of Jordan's pronouns, how to navigate the school system, and the power of gender performance. Despite the small size of this community, the McIntosh family and others were able to contribute to the larger community by providing educational workshops in their local library and educating school administrators on professional development opportunities about LGBTQ+ issues (inclusive of pronouns and gender expression). On the outside, it seemed as if the larger community was making an effort to understand these children and their families. However, a small fraction of teachers and families were making it difficult for these students to live their authentic lives in a productive learning environment.

This year, Jordan would be entering the ninth grade at Oakton High School. Many of the students who attended Oakton had also attended elementary and middle school with Jordan, so many were accustomed to seeing Jordan not in typical male clothes or presenting typical masculine behaviors. However, there remained several students, teachers, and staff who were unfamiliar with using Jordan's pronouns or even unwilling to take the time to get to know Jordan. Before the first day of school, the McIntosh family sat down and discussed whether to have a teacher conference to provide teachers and administrators with resources. Madison asked, "What are your thoughts, Jordan?"

Jordan responded hesitantly, "Well, I would like to begin the academic year with a clean slate and try to be my own advocate. Thank you both for always going to school with me, but I am in high school now, and I want to try to do this on my own. Besides, I don't want folks to get the wrong impression that I need my moms to come in and take care of me all the time," they finished with a smirk.

The family agreed that Jordan would handle the first few weeks of their first year in high school on their own—for now. If a conflict arose within the first two to three months, the family would convene a conference with all Jordan's teachers and administrators if necessary.

For Jordan, the first day of school almost resembled a family reunion for students. It was always an opportunity to reconnect with folks you knew from your past and connect with new people, including teachers. Jordan's first class of the day was health education, which students in their district were required to take for graduation. What drew Jordan to the course was the course description, which stated the following:

> The objective of this course is to introduce learners to the word "health" and the implications of this global concept. By understanding this word and its implications, learners will then take on a global understanding of what health disparities mean and their application to the world in which learners live. By the end of the course, learners will create and evaluate the meaning of health, living a healthy lifestyle, and participating in/cultivating a community for all.

Jordan knew immediately that this would be the course for them because they wanted to continue to help build the community that had supported them and their parents through elementary and middle school. Jordan struggled with questions like "What does health mean?" "How does my racial background affect my well-being?" and "Who makes the decisions on whether or not I am leading a healthy lifestyle?" This was the course that sang to Jordan's soul!

The person teaching the course was Ms. Dickson. She had been teaching this course for the past five years and had been a teacher in the school system for 20 years. Ms. Dickson was a decorated teacher, having received the Teacher of Year Award for the district twice and been nominated for Most Innovative Teacher of Year when she first started teaching 20 years ago. Ms. Dickson was the most sought-after health teacher in the entire school because of how she engaged the students and taught the concepts. One of her projects for the class was to have students get into pairs and care for an egg for three weeks. The students' objectives for this project were to observe the egg; negotiate how the pair would spend time with the egg; address activities the pair would do with the egg (if possible); and get to know the other person taking care of the egg better outside of the classroom (if possible). The student pairs were always male and female.

Despite the success Ms. Dickson had in the classroom, her traditional two-heterosexual-binary-parent views on gender roles, expression, and pronoun use had filtered into her classroom throughout the years without being addressed. Ms. Dickson was adamant that boys are boys and girls are girls (a binary worldview) and should be treated as such by using their traditional pronouns. For Ms. Dickson, going into the new academic year would not be any different, even though it would bring her first interaction with someone like Jordan. Boys are boys, and girls are girls.

"Good morning, everyone, and welcome to our first day of school and our first health class, 'Health Education and the World Around Us.' My name is Ms. Dickson, and I will be your teacher for this academic year. I want to start today off by going around the room. Please tell me your name and something we should know about you!" Ms. Dickson exclaimed. When their turn came, Jordan thought to themselves that this was the opportunity to set the tone for the year! This was it. Ms. Dickson said, "Jordan McIntosh?"

Jordan stood up and said, "I'm here. My name is Jordan McIntosh, and something about me you should know is that I use *they/them* pronouns." Ms. Dickson was astonished. This was the first time this distinguished teacher had had in her classroom a student who was marked/identified male on her attendance school records, was wearing fingernail polish, and had a bit of a flamboyant air. Maybe she had simply never noticed this in previous classes; maybe she noticed now because it was a Black child standing up in her class stating this. This was something different. "Am I a *racist* because I just noticed Jordan's race and not his . . . their . . . What is *its* pronoun?" Ms. Dickson thought. There was an awkward silence after Jordan made their statement, and Ms. Dickson noticed that she was staring at her student. She blinked and said, "Very well, Jordan, it is a pleasure to meet you," with half a smile.

Jordan smiled, said, "Thank you, and I am really excited about this class!" and sat down. "This is not so bad," Jordan thought. "I did it on my own and advocated for myself." The remainder of the first day of school went just as smoothly as Jordan's first class. Everyone seemed accepting and welcoming. Even though Jordan did not think every teacher was rooting for them, it felt good to be heard and seen in the classroom.

In the teacher's lounge, Ms. Dickson discussed her interaction with Jordan with her colleague and friend, history teacher Mr. Buchanan, asking for his thoughts: "He just stood right up and said, 'My name is Jordan, and I use *they/them* pronouns.' What does that even mean? Are we all of the sudden supposed to change the English language to fit the needs of the few? I just don't get it!"

Mr. Buchanan responded, "Marie, the world is changing, and, historically, the English language was created by white men."

"Joe, I didn't come to you for a history lesson. This is about how one child, a teenager, could possibly destroy the beginning of a community by influencing others with *his* confusing identity," Ms. Dickson snapped.

"Do you want my honest opinion, Marie, or not?" questioned Mr. Buchanan. Ms. Dickson nodded her head yes.

Mr. Buchanan went on: "Let the child express *themself*. By not creating an environment for them to grow and learn, you are doing more harm than good. Think about it. Besides, you have accomplished so much in your teaching career. Are you really going to get upset about a child making a decision about their pronouns? Is this about the child, or is this about you, Marie?"

"Well, I just believe that boys should act like boys and girls should act like girls. The topic I cover in the classroom is so easy to explain because it is black and white," explained Ms. Dickson.

"Is it really, Marie? I may not know your subject matter, but if anything is more complicated than history, it is the topic of health!" They both chuckled at Mr. Buchanan's remark. But Ms. Dickson still felt an unwavering need to take a stand in her classroom. Was this student, Jordan McIntosh, now going to set a precedent for her current and future classes?

Jordan had a fantastic first day of school, and the weeks that followed seemed to be the same, but Ms. Dickson did not interact with Jordan the same way she interacted with the other students. Ms. Dickson stumbled over Jordan's pronouns continually and at times would just stare at them when the class was doing a seated assignment or group activity. The worst part was that other students started to pick up on how Jordan was being treated differently in class. Jordan thought it was just their imagination until Alicia, Jordan's best friend and classmate, said something one day while they were walking home after school. "Jordan, do you notice how Ms. Dickson treats you a little different?" asked Alicia.

"What do you mean?" responded Jordan naively.

"I mean . . . ever since the first day of school, Ms. Dickson stumbles over your pronouns or can't even get your name right. It's Jordan! Not Jonathan or James or Jasmine or Jacob. I notice how she stares at your fingernail polish, your clothes, your hair. She just stares at you like . . . It's a little creepy."

"Maybe she is jealous of my ensemble. I mean I am the most fabulously dressed person in our school!" Both students giggled, but sadness loomed over Jordan's face. "I just wanted to be able to be me in our school and advocate for me without my parents having to get involved," continued Jordan.

"Well, you have put up with enough. You are doing well in her class; it is just that she does not treat you fairly. She never calls on you. She avoids your questions. She practically jumps when you approach her," detailed Alicia. "Jordan, we have to do something."

"We?" asked Jordan.

"We have been best friends forever, and we cannot have this one teacher destroy your first year of high school. So what do you say?" asked Alicia.

Jordan nodded their head in agreement. "I can't continue feeling like I'm in limbo with her. I know teachers don't have to like everyone they teach, but don't they have to at least respect their students?"

Alicia countered, "Point made, my friend, but let's say in her mind she thinks she *is* respecting you. Then what?"

"A conversation must be had with Ms. Dickson. I think it is time to involve my parents," replied Jordan.

Two months of the school year had gone by when Alicia and Jordan spoke with Jordan's parents and the support group the McIntosh family belonged to, to help facilitate discussions about what it means to be a part of the LGBTQ+ community, pronoun use, and gender education. After speaking with the school's principal, the teens organized an LGBTQ+ and allies club to help facilitate these conversations and educate others on the difference between being a bystander and being an advocate. After all, research shows that having LGBTQ+ clubs in schools helps prevent suicidal ideation and helps overall mental health of those who identify, even if they never go to the club (Truong et al. 2021). By the third month of school, the students worked with the school to develop a homeroom lesson with teachers for National Coming Out Day (October 11). This did not go over well, because the principal felt many teachers would not be comfortable with the topic. The principal proposed an assembly instead. The students also began advocacy through making presentations and writing letters to the school board and local government agencies as to why pronouns matter.

As Jordan and Alicia were walking down the hall one day, they overheard a familiar voice say, "Why can't these students just come to school and leave the politics to the adults?" The voice belonged to Ms. Dickson," and Jordan McIntosh had had enough of what felt like hatred but could also be a lack of understanding on the part of Ms. Dickson. With a booming voice, Jordan immediately responded, "It is because of people like you who try to silence people like me. You will never understand the pain you put me through, Ms. Dickson, and it's time for you to become the student to better understand how your views are negatively affecting the student community." Her mouth wide open, Ms. Dickson pushed through the halls with a flushed face.

Key Takeaways and Concluding Thoughts

Being Black and navigating gender identity, gender expression, and sexual identity are the main focus for this case study. Jordan's parents are two women, and Jordan's pronouns are *they/them*. Ms. Dickson is a "traditional" health education teacher in that she puts forward her belief system of families being male and female taking care of a child (or an egg, in this case). She has a hard time navigating pronoun use and does not understand why students can't keep to the "traditional" way things were. She causes harm to Jordan, whether consciously or subconsciously, through how she treats them. Examples included are using heteronormative views and projects in health education class, not being flexible to there being more than one way have a family, having rigid views on gender identity and gender roles, staring at Jordan and making them feel uncomfortable, and not using Jordan's pronouns. As Mr. Buchanan shares in the case, "By not creating an environment for them to grow and learn, [such teachers] are doing them more harm." The principal further illustrates white normative or supremacy culture by not pursuing homeroom lessons because teachers would not be "comfortable with the content." However, the principal does permit the students and Jordan's family to educate and advocate through a school assembly.

Discussion Questions

1. What steps would you take to create an inclusive classroom?
2. How can health educators build a more inclusive curriculum and more inclusive instructional practices?
3. As a teacher, how can you take steps to position the material as the foundation of what you are teaching?
4. What changes could best support the students in this case study?
5. What role did Mr. Buchanan play in naming the harm happening to Jordan in this case study?
6. If you overheard the interaction between Jordan and Ms. Marie Dickson in the hallway, what would your response to the individuals be?
7. How are gender and gender performance reinforced by society?

References and Suggested Resources

Bannister, M.E. 2020. "School Library as a Safe Harbor for LGBTQ Students and Families." *Knowledge Quest* 48 (3): E1-E6.

Brown, C., H. Frohard-Dourlent, B.A. Wood, E. Saewyc, M.E. Eisenberg, and C.M. Porta. 2020. "'It Makes Such a Difference': An Examination of How LGBTQ Youth Talk About Personal Gender Pronouns." *Journal of the American Association of Nurse Practitioners* 32 (1): 70-80.

Earnshaw, V.A., D.D. Menino, L.M. Sava, J. Perrotti, J., T.N. Barnes, D.L. Humphrey, and S.L. Reisner. 2020. "LGBTQ Bullying: A Qualitative Investigation of Student and School Health Professional Perspectives." *Journal of LGBT Youth* 17 (3): 280-297.

Johnson, I.R., E.S. Pietri, D.M. Buck, and R. Daas. 2021. "What's in a Pronoun: Exploring Gender Pronouns as an Organizational Identity-Safety Cue Among Sexual and Gender Minorities." *Journal of Experimental Social Psychology* 97:104-194.

Manion, J. 2018. "The Performance of Transgender Inclusion." *Public Seminar*, November 27, 2018. https://publicseminar.org/essays/the-performance-of-trans-gender-inclusion/.

McGlashan, H., and K. Fitzpatrick. 2017. "LGBTQ Youth Activism and School: Challenging Sexuality and Gender Norms." *Health Education* 117 (5): 485-497.

Moser, C., and M. Devereux. 2019. "Gender Neutral Pronouns: A Modest Proposal." *International Journal of Transgenderism* 20 (2-3): 331.

Truong, N., C. Clark, S. Rosenbach, and J. Kosciw. 2021. *The GSA Study: Results of National Surveys About Students' and Advisors' Experiences in Gender and Sexuality Alliance Clubs.* New York: GLSEN. www.glsen.org/sites/default/files/2021-12/GLSEN_ResearchInstitute_GSAStudy_12012021.pdf.

Webb, A., E. Matsuno, S. Budge, M. Krishnan, and K. Balsam. 2016. "Nonbinary Gender Identities: Fact Sheet." www.apadivisions.org/division-44/resources/nonbinary-fact-sheet.pdf.

9

"Pull Yourself Up by Your Bootstraps"

Anika Thrower

The sounds of crickets get louder and louder as Maxine sleepily silences her phone alarm, making another fruitless mental note. For the 10th time, she promises herself to change her annoying alarm tone. Maxine hoists herself out of bed and starts her morning routine, listening to the morning news while brewing her coffee. "Overnight on the quiet streets of Manchester, neighbors heard shots ring out," the Channel Eight news anchor announces somberly.

"Another senseless death due to a rival gang dispute at a basketball court. When will the madness end?" Maxine questions. "We have to keep these boys active," she murmurs softly under her breath and moves forward with her routine.

As she leaves the bathroom, she catches her reflection in the full-length mirror. Stopping at attention, Maxine runs her hands over her sides and down her hips, acknowledging her hard work. Looking back at her from the mirror is a vivid image of her cousin Lue-Lue giving her a high five. Next Tuesday will be her 15th anniversary of being a bona fide runner. Her mind races back to Sundays and how she would see Lue-Lue. "Who said Black girls don't run?" she shouts as she sashays away from the mirror. Scurrying off to her bedroom, Maxine throws on her running attire, rushes down the stairs, grabs her reflector vest, ear buds, and cell phone, and then slams the door behind her. Realizing she is a few minutes behind schedule, she sprints down the middle of the foggy street.

Running up the winding hills on the South Side of Pittsburgh in the early morning during the autumn months is usually refreshing, but today the wind pushes against her. Eating the Mount Washington hills is not easy after a night of enjoying her neighbor's sugar cookies, so she decides to bring out the big guns. A lover of music, Maxine cues up old-school mixes with Earth, Wind & Fire to serenade her first mile. The smooth sounds instantly take her back to the lazy Sunday afternoons of her youth. Sundays were special to her because the adults in her life seemed more laid-back and happier then. In a family full of female caregivers, it was special to Maxine to see her uncles around on Sundays because it was their day off. Having the males aside from her own father present in her life—whether it was fixing a bike tire, working on a car, or simply being around—meant something.

While running, Maxine reminisces about her childhood. Even back then, she enjoyed listening to the music from cars creeping down the streets of the North Side of Pittsburgh with her cousins. Maxine recalled playing hopscotch with neighborhood kids, sipping ice ball cups, and smelling the chicken frying from her grandmother's kitchen window. Life was simple then.

She recalls one particular summer Sunday afternoon when she was 12 years old. She saw a shapely, tall Black woman listening to her Walkman and jogging down North Avenue. Seeing her was peculiar because she usually only saw white people jogging and walking in the early mornings on her way to school. "Black people run?" she asked herself. "I have only seen folks running in an emergency." One of her uncles noticed Maxine staring at the woman in motion and told her the woman was her second cousin Lucy. Maxine shot him a side-eye look in disbelief. To prove it, he hollered, "Hey, hey, Lue-Lue, I see you!" Lucy looked over at them and hollered back with an upward head nod, "Hey, Charlie." Maxine did not know anyone Black who intentionally exercised outside of school activities. Of course, she had brothers and cousins who played basketball for fun. But Lue-Lue looked like she enjoyed exercising—so that was different.

After that day, she began to notice her big cousin Lue-Lue jogging on many Sundays. Later that summer, Maxine and Lue-Lue became acquainted at a family picnic. Lue-Lue, a well-respected lawyer on the South Side of Pittsburgh who had several friends and connections, took a liking to Maxine because she had no kids of her own. Hoping to plant seeds, her big cousin slowly introduced Maxine to the rec league tennis and volleyball teams for adult women. Maxine served as the volleyball team's first water girl, building relationships of her own. As they got used to seeing Maxine tagging along with Lue-Lue more and more, the other players would ask, "So, young lady, what do you want to be when you grow up?" Over time she was introduced to other girls her age who loved sports too. Through a mix of sports and relationships, Maxine was introduced to new experiences, and over the years, she developed lasting connections with other females and males of all races through a mutual love of team sports. Of all the activities she participated in with Lue-Lue and others, her first love remained running.

Refocusing on her run, Betty Wright's song *"Tonight Is the Night"* blaring in her ears, Maxine reaches the steep hill's summit and makes her way down Grandview Avenue, the wind now behind her. Looking across the river, she sees the bright lights from the scenic area of the city called the Point. On top of Mount Washington is where the colony of busy bees moves about. Busy bees are what she calls the several dozen runners she's informally become acquainted with over the last few years. There are singles, couples, and small and large groups of joggers and runners of all ages—mostly white people. Maxine is one of the few sistas among the colony of busy bees.

After her run, Maxine peels off her wet clothes, showers, and gets ready for work. Her mind darts to the landscape of the semester, running over the upcoming shift into discussing racial inequalities in one of her classes at a small community college on the outskirts of Pittsburgh. As a 38-year-old college professor, Maxine enjoys lecturing. After all, it has been her life's work to spread awareness to the newer generation of educators teaching health studies in urban public schools such as the ones she attended. She is three weeks into her cultural awareness classes and plans a deep dive into social justice themes. Through formal and informal conversations with these soon-to-be teachers, Maxine has found a seeming lack of knowledge regarding the life of urban youth that she finds alarming.

Maxine's small group of working-class, typically white women students ranges in age from 22 to 45 years old. If they are to become these children's role models, there is work to be done! Historically, the shift into racial inequalities has made some of her students uneasy. In many instances, these well-meaning individuals are unaware of the intricate lives of urban youth outside of the classroom setting. Thinking back to the latest shooting, she feels her eyes begin to water. From Maxine's perspective, teachers have considerable voids to help fill. In addition, she feels it is essential to ensure that children are exposed to as many activities, such as team sports, as possible in order to build self-esteem.

Maxine gathers the items she needs for her long day on campus. She murmurs to herself, "Focus, Maxi!" She is determined not to forget anything this time. Her drive to work is usually relaxing, especially during autumn. Fall means the changing of the leaves, and seeing the parade of brilliant colors makes her smile. Upon entering her classroom on campus, she sees Justin, one of two males taking her course that semester, sitting in his regular seat in a back corner next to the window overlooking the river. He and Maxine exchange pleasantries. Justin is following his usual habit of silently enjoying breakfast and drinking a hot beverage. She can tell he is a physically active, mild-mannered, methodic individual. He usually uses this time to center himself before the other students come into class.

After a few minutes, the cohort of students starts sporadically shuffling into the classroom. This cohort is comprised of mostly white women, one Black woman, two Hispanic women, and two white males. The white males are Justin and Evan. In all, she has 25 students in this class, which to Maxine's delight is offered in the early morning. She enjoys how the students are generally ready to hit the ground learning, whether through heavy lecturing or facilitated dialogue. Each semester, she makes it a point to get to know something unique about each of her students. She values connections and supporting them through their teaching assignments. After all, she knows the jobs of the future teachers will hold more than meets the eyes. Unbeknownst to them, they have a special responsibility to care for the youth in the most vulnerable areas of the City of Pittsburgh. Maxine is her community's keeper; therefore, she is her students' keeper.

"Good morning, all," Maxine says with a welcoming smile as she stands in front of the class.

"Good morning, Professor Phillips," most students respond in unison.

She begins: "Within the last weeks, we deliberated on some of the fundamental attributes teachers and the school environment should possess. As we all agreed, being nurturers and holding spaces for our scholars to flourish are the keys to success. Today, let us shift our focus to our students' home lives. Put your student-teaching assignments, procedure, books, and learning outcomes aside, and ponder on this question: 'How does home life look for the students you interact with?'"

The classroom is quiet for several seconds. Maxine is determined to solicit feedback prior to moving forward. This wave of silence might be uncomfortable for some instructors, but not for her; she has been here before. She plants herself on her desk, takes a sip of her water, and waits for replies.

"Can we make assertions?" Maxine asks. "Let us start here. Can we name some things on the home front needed to support our students' learning?"

"Breakfast?" Brandi says hurriedly.

"Yes, Brandi, balanced meals are helpful," Maxine affirms. "Anyone else?"

"A restful night of sleep," Connie says confidently.

"Supportive parents," Evan mentions.

"Thank you for your input, everyone," Maxine continues. "How many of you have heard of the cycle of poverty? What do you think that means?"

Evan shares, "People who are poor stay poor? It just goes over and over again?"

"What else do we think about when we hear 'cycle of poverty'?" Maxine asks.

Brandi shares, "I guess it would be hard to do stuff like sports and clubs if your parents can't pay for you to do them."

"Yes, that is another great factor to consider," says Maxine. "What about access to college, trade school, and so on?"

Justin shares, "It might be hard to pay for college if your family is focused on affording food and paying rent."

"Yes, these are some of the constraints that bind people in a cycle of poverty," Maxine shares. "As a result, think about this as we are delving into our projects: Having an idea about the lives of our students outside of class is a valid consideration. Since we are responsible for their education, we must be informed. In addition, as educators, we must understand how their home environments affect their learning and to what degree poverty may be a driving constraint in access to basic needs being met—this is important. Being an ally in their learning means being an ally in their overall well-being."

Maxine describes the project the cohort will work on in the upcoming weeks. This assignment challenges them to consider how their students' well-being looks outside of scholastics and within the home environment. In short, they are tasked with picking three students to observe over the next few weeks. Data will be collected through informal conversations, group activities, and overhearing students talk among themselves. The project is personal for Maxine. After all, she is responsible for imparting insights to future educators. Such understandings will help the cohort develop their students' intellectual and holistic well-being and see why there are so many challenges based on the cycle of poverty.

"How does well-being look outside the classroom?" asks Maxine. Some students look at each other blankly while others shuffle through their notes.

Maxine's mind starts to wander, thinking back to her upbringing. As a young girl, she loved numbers. Since math was her favorite subject, followed by science, her classmates called her Whiz Kid. Maxine had teachers who cared about her general well-being as well. Nevertheless, she wished exercise outside of recess was emphasized. Sure, she saw statuesque Black women such as Jackie Joyner-Kersee running track and field during the Olympics. But not seeing a Black woman run or even exercise in her community until she was 10 years old seemed like a crime. Why didn't other Black people in her community, or even in her own family, choose some form of exercise? Maxine wants to change that trajectory for youth.

"I know we are moving into new territory and, seemingly, away from a teacher's job description," Maxine says with a light chuckle, "but let us think of our students as customers. We need to know their needs, and what barriers they have to accessing basic needs and extracurricular opportunities. In that way, we can be more effective in educating the leaders of tomorrow. Let us map out the attributes which could provide the lion's share of the information needed to make educated assertions about the lives of our students outside of classes."

During the latter part of the class, she provides demographic data to give the future teachers a better understanding of the communities they work in. Although Maxine grew up in the urban North Side of Pittsburgh, she knows where every farmers' market and pizzeria is located.

Most of the low-income neighborhoods in Pittsburgh are urban, and one of the biggest employers is University of Pittsburgh. Depending on the neighborhood, the socioeconomic status could change from borough to borough and even block to block. Black students usually come from single-parent households where their mothers are most likely unmarried and heads of their households. Maxine will send her amateur investigators into schools within the neighborhoods of Fox Chapel, Beltzhoover, Monroeville, Manchester, Northview Heights, Garfield, Northside, and Oakland. By the end of class, the cohort understands their project.

Maxine announces to the class, "After Thanksgiving break, I would like each one of you to come back with a one-page essay about how things are going, so be ready to verbally present an informal update. Before I dismiss everyone, are there any questions?" Reading the room, she sees that everyone seems set, quietly talking among themselves, except Justin and Evan. Unlike their peers, they look confused.

"Okay, see everyone next week," says Maxine. "Evan and Justin, could you both stay back for a few minutes?" Once the classroom is empty, Maxine walks closer to the two students sitting in the back.

"How do you guys feel about the assignment?" she asks.

"Professor Phillips, I can speak for myself only. I do not know if Justin feels the same." Evan pauses, then clears his throat. "I care about the kids I teach, but I just want to be the best teacher. Should we be getting involved in the personal lives of students?"

Maxine looks at Justin, who sits tapping his pen on his desk. "Justin, any thoughts?" she asks, upbeat yet internally concerned.

"No," Justin says.

"Evan, I see how you could feel that way," says Maxine. She continues, "Okay, in addition to collecting the information as stated, I want you both to home in on the household composition of your students. Who are the heads of the households? Specifically, are the families coming from two-parent, single-mother, or single-father households? Are they being raised by uncles, grandparents, or who? Have their families lived in that neighborhood for generations?"

In unison, they both agree, but Justin still seems a little hesitant.

"I look forward to learning what you both uncover. Come see me during office hours if either one of you needs support," Maxine says, and then dismisses them both. Evan gathers his things and leaves. Maxine sits at her desk in the front of the class, watching Justin slowly get his personal items together. She notes his body language and, picking up on his hesitance to leave, decides to probe his thoughts.

"May I ask how you feel about this project? Most students use this project to dig in a bit and learn more about their students' life experiences outside of the classroom setting. What you learn could be a game changer and could allow your teaching techniques to adapt to being more relatable," Maxine remarks.

"I get it," Justin says hesitantly.

"Go on, Justin. You can speak openly," encourages Maxine.

"Professor Phillips, a problem I routinely encounter is that with my students—well, mostly with preteen males—they state I am not their father whenever they are redirected. I want to do a good job teaching and have wanted to be a teacher my whole life. But I struggle with being relatable. How do I begin to help them develop holistically when I sometimes feel like an imposter in their world? Sometimes they do not acknowledge my presence!" Justin sighs in frustration but keeps his composure and continues softly, "I am a white male born and raised in Squirrel Hill. I cannot change who I am and should not have to. How can I be more relatable to the Black male students when I am white?"

Tilting her head to the side and hoping to plant a seed, Maxine asks, "Do you like sports?"

"I love sports. I grew up playing any sport imaginable," Justin says enthusiastically.

"Great, let's start there," Maxine remarks, laughing out loud.

"Huh?" smiles Justin.

After her conversation with Justin and teaching another class, Maxine has a quick lunch with a colleague. Her day on campus concludes with attending a department meeting. She thinks about taking an express yoga class later on. Ensuring that she has all of her belongings, Maxine leaves campus for the day. Walking to her car slowly, she notes the cool fall air and once again enjoys the crunching of the brilliantly colored leaves under her loafers.

After getting into her car, she turns on the radio: "As an update to last night's gang-related shooting . . . " Maxine changes the radio station and stops when she hears some smooth holiday jazz. "Can we get past Thanksgiving first?" she asks the radio. Then her thoughts flood back to the concerns Justin raised, because they are all too real. Her own involvement in sports at such a young age provided her with the stability and structure she needed once her parents divorced. She realizes that being middle class enabled her to access opportunities that others could not. With Maxine's mom raising her and three boys, life was not easy. The lack of her mom's presence was felt. However, she knew her mother was working all the hours she could on three jobs to ensure that the lights stayed on. At the age of 12, she caught her mother sobbing in the late night. Frightened, she asked why she was crying, and the only thing Mom said was "Sometimes you got to pull yourself up by the bootstrap. Thank goodness I have the boots to pull up." Some of her classmates growing up in the projects didn't have a boot to pull on. It was at times like this that she put more energy into sports.

Unbeknownst to her at the time, sports made her more focused in school and kept her away from some of the pitfalls other girls her age experienced.

Four weeks later, Maxine walks into class and sees Justin as usual, but except for a dry smile, his energy is different. Maxine puts her things on her desk and sits quietly sipping her coffee. Shortly, her other students walk in and take their seats. Once most students are seated, class begins.

"How has everyone been doing?" Maxine asks. "Did you enjoy your Thanksgiving break?" Most everyone nods.

She continues, "Your final assignment is not due yet; however, today you are tasked with checking in and reporting about your progress. I would like to see if there are common themes and assertions you are starting to formulate."

One after another, her students report about their experiences. Maxine takes notes as each student speaks. She is delighted to see her students' willingness to get to know their pupils outside of the classroom. Some students really own the project and mention how some of their pupils' attitudes have changed, and how they seem to want to do better with class assignments. They also mention an uptick in test grades. Some common themes are lack of structure in the household, broken homes, kids raising their siblings, food insecurity, hints of abuse, and even homelessness. Most of the students' families the college students teach have been in the same neighborhood for generations, which makes the students feel that there is a link to the cycle of poverty. They do not have access to paid extracurricular activities, and some of them have shared that they have to work to help pay for house bills while others have shared that they had to take care of their younger brothers and sisters. One of Maxine's students mentions a situation where a 12-year-old-boy is being raised by his single mother. With money being tight, he is contemplating making some "side cash" to tide the family over.

"All of these things are real issues, and though daunting, it's best to know what your students are dealing with outside the classroom," Maxine says. She then continues softly, while examining her notes and repositioning herself atop her desk, "I am looking forward to everyone's final project and debrief!" She says, "Justin, we did not hear your update."

"Professor Phillips," Justin says softly, "my experience"—he clears his throat—"has not been typical, so I'd rather wait until I have more data."

"What's going on, Justin? Your peers and I are here to support you," Maxine responds, stepping toward Justin. By this time, all 24 of Justin's classmates are quietly looking at him.

Justin begins, "Things were going well. Really well, in fact. I took your advice and started to meet the boys where they were. I could not get them to stop talking about sports. I've never seen such a bunch of die-hard Steelers fans!" Taking a big gulp, he continues, "Until their teacher, Mr. Shafer, died, I mean passed away, in his sleep right before Thanksgiving break."

Everyone gasps, with a few "Oh my God" murmurs filling the classroom.

With tears welling in his eyes, Justin says, "That's when I learned how many of those guys, I mean young men, have no fathers at home. Literally!" Justin says, sniffing, with tears streaming. "For many of them, Mr. Shafer was their father."

Maxine wants to walk over to Justin, embrace him, and encourage him to let it all out. But she stays still, listens, and simply provides a safe space for him.

Drying his eyes on his sleeve and looking straight ahead, Justin continues, "These low-income kids need me!" Looking around and making eye contact with several of his peers, with a quivering voice he continues, "These young men need . . . "

Thinking back to the impact Cousin Lue-Lue had in her life and fighting back her own tears, Maxine finishes his sentence: "Us. Justin, it's going to take a village, and they need us."

Key Takeaways and Concluding Thoughts

In this case study, Maxine, a college professor, shared her experiences as a middle-class Black woman leading a mostly white group of future teachers. She guided students to review the cycle of poverty by having students investigate the socioeconomic environment and social determinants of health and interview some of their students. Maxine reflected on her upbringing, the stereotypes of being Black, and how little people run for exercise in the community. Her influence empowered her own family members to think differently about Black stereotypes and exercise.

It is vital that health educators reflect on their own identity based on where they are in the intersectionality components and how that is similar to or different from the students they serve. Maxine is Black and most of the students she worked with in the college were white. Most of the preservice teachers were white, and the students they served were Black, Indigenous, and people of color. Through the investigation, students were able to unpack some of the cycle of poverty and social determinants of health linked to those with lack of access to paid extracurricular activities, single-parent households, and other barriers to opportunities (e.g., being unable to afford college, having to work or care for siblings) that the white preservice teachers took for granted in their upbringing.

Discussion Questions

1. What influences were present for Maxine that influenced her to be a role model for others?
2. Within this case study, students were charged with providing a briefing of their findings halfway through their project. What

additional findings or themes linked to the cycle of poverty do you think they will have discovered once the final projects are done?

3. Before Justin returned to class to discuss the passing of the teacher he was shadowing, he struggled with being more relatable to his students. Think back to your own education. Can you recall a teacher who was unrelatable and unable to connect and build relationships with students? If the teacher had been at least slightly more relatable, do you think you would have done better in the class?

4. What are some immediate next steps for Justin to consider as he works to complete his teaching assignment effectively and help his students through this difficult time?

5. If applicable, think about your own pedagogy. How can you become more relatable to students, especially those students who seemingly struggle?

6. Do you use collaborative learning activities to foster community in your classroom? If so, describe feedback from your students.

7. Is it possible for a white teacher to be as effective in instructing Black students as a Black teacher is?

Suggested Resources

Bonner, F.A, II. 2014. *Building on Resilience: Models and Frameworks of Black Male Success Across the P-20 Pipeline*. Illustrated edition. New York City: Routledge.

Bowe, F. 2016. *Life Skills for Tweens: How to Cook, Make Friends, Be Self Confident and Healthy. Everything a Pre Teen Should Know to Be a Brilliant Teenager*. Bemberton Limited.

Burrell, M., A. White, L. Frerichs, M. Funchess, C. Cerulli, L. DiGiovanni, and K. Hassmiller. 2021. "Depicting 'the System': How Structural Racism and Disenfranchisement in the United States Can Cause Dynamics in Community Violence Among Males in Urban Black Communities." *Social Science & Medicine* 272 (March).

Daniel Tatum, B. 2003. *"Why Are All the Black Kids Sitting Together in the Cafeteria?"* New York: Basic Books.

Duque, R.B. "Black Health Matters Too … Especially in the Era of Covid-19: How Poverty and Race Converge to Reduce Access to Quality Housing, Safe Neighborhoods, and Health and Wellness Services and Increase the Risk of Co-morbidities Associated with Global Pandemics." *Journal of Racial and Ethnic Health Disparities* 8:1012-1025. https://doi.org/10.1007/s40615-020-00857-w.

Goodwin, B. 2022. *The New Classroom Instruction That Works: The Best Research-Based Strategies for Increasing Student Achievement*. Alexandria, VA: Association for Supervision & Curriculum Development.

Noguera, P.A. (2011). "A Broader and Bolder Approach Uses Education to Break the Cycle of Poverty." *Phi Delta Kappan* 93(3): 8-14. https://doi.org/10.1177/003172171109300303.

Scherer, M. 2016. *On Poverty and Learning: Readings from Educational Leadership (EL Essentials)*. Alexandria, VA: Association for Supervision & Curriculum Development.

Schwanke, J. 2022. *The Teacher's Principal: How School Leaders Can Support and Motivate Their Teachers*. Alexandria, VA: Association for Supervision & Curriculum Development.

Wood, L.J., and S.R. Harper. 2015. *Advancing Black Male Student Success From Preschool Through Ph.D.* New York City: Routledge.

Yendol-Hoppey, D. 2019. *The Reflective Educator's Guide to Classroom Research: Learning to Teach and Teaching to Learn Through Practitioner Inquiry*. 4th rev. ed. Thousand Oaks, CA: Corwin.

CASE STUDY
10

"It's Time to Eat!"

Victor Ramsey

During health education class at a high school in Brooklyn, New York City, students were learning about comparing and contrasting the benefits of and barriers to practicing a variety of healthy behaviors. Specifically, there were discussions from a lesson on food deserts in which students made connections between some of their experiences of the food they ate, the cost of the food, and food shortage that either they or their extended family and friends had in the recent past. Food justice, food deserts, and poverty were the focus of heated debates during this class. The experiences the students shared were meaningful and allowed a realistic connection to the lesson.

Mr. Hewitt began the class with a bell ringer on the board as students entered that asked them to define a food desert. Several students laughed and shouted, "There are no deserts in Brooklyn!" Mr. Hewitt prompted them to think about what a desert is and how it can be linked with food. "Would you have a lot of food in a desert?" he asked. Students' brainstormed responses included issues pertaining to the disparities, inequalities, and political ramifications associated with the lack of quality, nutritional foods in marginalized communities.

Carlos shared, "There is a bodega near me that makes the best breakfast sandwiches fresh." Bryce agreed and added, "But they only have bananas and no other fruits or vegetables that aren't in cans there." Reuben shared, "Yeah, it's because all the organic grocery stores and stuff are in different neighborhoods. Not our neighborhood." Mike shared, "That's because they don't want us to have those types of foods. It costs too much to have a big store like that by where we live."

They also debated about the difference between organic and nonorganic foods, specifically which is better and their comparative affordability. "I don't get why in America we have to choose between organic and nonorganic. Why are they putting all those chemicals in our foods and plants anyway?" said Carlos. Reuben shared, "They are trying to make money off of us, and they don't care about the quality of the produce or food. They only care about the quantity and the money they make off people."

Mr. Hewitt prompted the students to think about health literacy skills and advocacy in action in the community. This fostered the next part of the discussion, which delved into the Poor People's Campaign, a movement created on December 4, 1967, by the Southern Christian Leadership Conference (SCLC) to address unemployment, housing for the poor, and how poverty affects the lives of millions of Americans. The movement is spearheaded today by Bishop William J. Barber II, an American Protestant minister and social activist. He cochairs the Poor People's Campaign: A National Call for Moral Revival and is also a senior lecturer at Repairers of the Breach, another national movement committed to social change that trains and brings together people from all walks of life—activists, artists, and faith leaders—to organize and mobilize around a moral policy agenda to prioritize love, truth, and justice.

The featured documentary *Poor People's Campaign: A National Call for Moral Revival,* which shared the dismay of people from all walks of life, was a hot topic in class. After the discussion about the Poor People's Campaign and watching the documentary segment, students began to understand the power of food as a political and humanistic right for survival. Bryce shared, "Now I understand why we do not have the same resources that others with more money do in our neighborhood."

Mr. Hewitt prompted the students to think about what they do when they eat and how to advocate for improving food deserts. Some students shared that when they eat their meals their families talk about and pray for the less fortunate. Mike shared that he volunteers at a food bank in his community a few times a month with his mom and grandma. Carlos shared that his church has a food pantry where his family sometimes drops off food and sometimes picks food up. Mr. Hewitt responded that the work the students do at their churches and community centers helps bring more food justice to their community. The health education class helped the students understand challenges associated with access to food and ways to thrive and overcome food desert challenges—doing with less or finding and connecting with resources in their community, local government, churches, and other advocacy groups that can help.

The students discussed how many individuals they knew of who never had to worry about lack of food, food injustice, or any form of deprivation related to food or even housing. They talked about their families' experiences sharing food during traditional holidays and how food played an essential role in their lives.

Mr. Hewitt asked the students to think about social determinants of health related to food and culture. Reuben shared that he found this topic difficult to talk about sometimes as a first-generation person in the United States. Janine shared that her family came from Jamaica. Mr. Hewitt asked the students to think about stepping into the shoes of someone who is new to the country or recently immigrated and what benefits and challenges they may have. Mike said, "It depends on how much money they make, really. If you are broke, you can't afford the organic foods or the money to go get groceries further away or delivered to where you live." Janine said, "It was hard finding a good Jamaican grocery store that carried foods, fruits, and vegetables I was used to having in my home country."

Students felt comfortable sharing lived experiences of their families and journeys as immigrants and English language learners, especially since the stories were similar in many instances. For example, some students shared the challenges their families encountered when they first arrived in the United States or the lack of affordability of nutritious food.

Another food topic during health education class came from Bryant Terry's book *Black Food*, where he quotes Fannie Lou Hamer, an African American voting and women's rights activist, civil rights leader, community organizer, and cofounder and vice chair of the Freedom Democratic Party. Ms. Hamer articulated the vision of the Freedom Farm Cooperative, an agricultural cooperative, a rural economic development project, and a political organizing project that she founded in Mississippi in 1969. This project won scores of funders in its early days. Ms. Hamer said, "Food is necessary for survival. With the passage of the Voting Rights Act of 1965, I returned to Sunflower County, Mississippi and realized that the right to vote was insufficient for a healthy, happy, whole life. Voting does not include the right to access nutrient-rich food, safe and affordable housing, health care, and quality education" (Brooks & Hook, 2011). Students were empowered by this information and expressed their sentiments assertively during health class.

Mr. Hewitt transitioned the conversation to health literacy skills advocacy. After directing students to review a quote from a speech Fannie Lou Hamer gave in December 20, 1964—"I'm sick and tired of being sick and tired"—Mr. Hewitt asked the students what the quote means and what it means to be an advocate like Fannie Lou Hamer. Janine shared, "It sounds like she is always sick and always tired." Mr. Hewitt prompted for more. Reuben shared, "Being sick and tired may come from health and food." Mr. Hewitt said, "How can you be an advocate for better food conditions and access in school, at home, and in your neighborhoods? Talk to an elbow partner, and brainstorm possibilities and challenges in advocating."

Students worked for a few minutes, and Mr. Hewitt summarized their brainstorm before they left class.

The students transitioned to lunch period after health class. When students finished eating early, they could go to the gymnasium for physical activity opportunities, and a group of students went to play soccer games. This was one of the best times in their schedules, where they had opportunities to eat and share time together; they loved to build community through eating and playing. To see food as an aspect of the lives of the children we are entrusted to serve, love, and care for is important to health educators' understanding of how to improve our instructional practices. Food makes us happy during holidays and other events, so it is irrefutable that meaningful connections are made around food. The health education learning environment and other spaces within the school environment offer opportunities to connect with students. Students enjoy sharing their experiences and discussing topics related to food during their health education class sessions.

The next day in health education class, Mr. Hewitt reviewed healthy eating guidelines and shared pictures of food. Bryce and Carlos looked at each other and started laughing. Mr. Hewitt asked, "What's so funny, everyone?" Carlos answered, "The food you are showing is not what we eat in our houses. There are no rice, beans, plantains . . . nothing. That looks like white people food." "Yeah, Mr. Hewitt," said Bryce. "I don't see any collard greens or mac and cheese. I do see chicken, but we don't cook it like that. Where is the seasoning?" Taken aback, Mr. Hewitt stopped to think. He said, "You are right. This does look like just one way to eat. Maybe what we should do is go back to the nutrients and then change the activity to choose foods that match in pairs or groups. How does that sound?" The students agreed that this was better because they did not see themselves, their culture, or their families in the food pictures he was showing. Mr. Hewitt reframed the lesson for nutrients and healthy eating pattern overview by having the students build out plan for a week's worth of food that would match a healthy eating pattern based on nutrient-dense foods they enjoy in their homes.

Critical points noted during the discussions were how to address microaggressions and the challenges people from specific marginalized communities experience. By presenting only one type of "diet," who are we excluding and who are we saying is the "asset" or eating the "right" way—a dominant culture or norm? Janine and Melissa turned to Carlos and Bryce and thanked them for saying something. Carlos and Bryce shared that the visuals had made them feel that the food they eat at home was bad and that they too were bad for eating that way. Khadar shared, "The more we see the value and different types of food from other cultures, the more we learn about each other." Students shared that they were glad that these topics had come up with Mr. Hewitt and that he was flexible and reflective enough to recognize that he had only showed one way to eat nutrient-dense foods.

Health educators must not shy away from these difficult conversations; they must identify when they are wrong or creating a monolithic experience, admit when they are *not* presenting multiple perspectives and intersections, and be honest with their students about the reality of racism and microaggressions they may experience. After all, presenting that there is only one right way to do things is a white supremacy cultural norm. There are many ways across many cultures to eat healthy, nutrient-dense foods.

The students always looked forward to after-school activities. The school administrators allocated funding to provide meals for students who participated in after-school programs, many of whom looked forward to these meals because of the financial conditions in which they lived. The food at the after-school program was provided through a partnership between the school's food service and a community organization. The students' conversation was always filled with questions about what would be served and how much would be available to eat. The community where the school is located was ethnically and culturally different from the community the students came from, so the group expressed some anxiety about the choice of foods offered at the school. Some students commented that the food choices might not be of their preference because they were used to their ethnic foods. Others said that they never found the food choices at the school appealing. The food served where they were accustomed to eating and where everyone in the community came to get food was vastly different than what was served in the school.

It was exciting to see how relationships developed when these students came together to play sports and settled on what they would eat. Janine yelled, "Hey, let's try something new that the school is offering—something different!" Mike grumbled, "Yeah, but it's not what we like," and Melissa chimed in, "I can only imagine the taste of the food around here [referring to the community where the school is situated]. Oh, and y'all remember the conversation about food justice and food deserts that we had in health class?" Reuben commented, "I wonder if we will end up eating the dry-looking chicken and unseasoned vegetables from the pictures in Mr. Hewitt's class."

The students finally selected foods none of them had tried before at the school. They had a choice between vegetarian manicotti, lasagna, and a Mediterranean chicken pasta salad. Bryce chose the chicken pasta salad because he does not eat cheese or dairy. The others chose the vegetarian manicotti and lasagna. The collaborative process of sharing food that binds these relationships was evident once they agreed on what to eat. Some shared based on their dietary restrictions, preferences, and needs. They talked about the taste, the cost, and the fact that they could not afford to go to fancy restaurants or pay at places that served the food they were trying. Mike wondered, "Where do you buy this food anyway?" Khadar shared, "My family is celebrating Ramadan, so I can't eat and am fasting. But if I did, it would still need to match what my family says I can eat." After they played and ate, the students gave each other high fives and hugs and parted ways.

Key Takeaways and Concluding Thoughts

The most important thing in the world is family and love.

—John Wooden, former college and professional basketball coach and English teacher

John Wooden's quote resonates well with this case study because of the time the students spent together and bringing their cultures together. They interacted with other students, developed a nutrient-dense food plan from different cultures in Mr. Hewitt's health class, and tried new foods during after-school activities. Students made the connection between their own cultures and health education, saw how they could help make a difference in society, and practiced advocacy in their families and the communities where they live. Because Mr. Hewitt listened to Bryce and Carlos and pivoted to add voice for students to be seen, be heard, and share their cultures with others, students were elevated as assets in the health education class.

Food, food justice, and the nuances associated with food play a very important role in the lives of the children we teach. Educators, and health educators in particular, have the opportunity to address topics related to food and the culture and families of their students. *Culture* describes behaviors we can observe and those that are under the surface. These include traditions, dress, language, music, communication styles, and, yes, food. Culture influences how we perceive and respond to the world around us and how we learn in various situations at home, at school, with peers, and in the community.

Commonalities in collectivist communities can bring together diverse people of color and food can be the catalyst. Identifying differences between individualistic American culture and collectivist communities is important for leading health education toward an asset-based focus where all students are seen and valued. If teachers plan with their students in mind, students' ethnic foods can add value to a well-established class on food topics. Commonalities can bring students together, and learning and respecting the differences that each culture brings to the classroom are essential in fostering a healthy learning environment.

In this situation, Mr. Hewitt had a good class relationship where students felt comfortable speaking up and sharing that what he presented did not represent them and their cultures. Mr. Hewitt did not become defensive, but was open to the feedback and acted upon it to serve and bring in the voice and cultures of his students within the framework of the health objective. He helped students see that although one resource may have a dominant representation, you can take the parameters (e.g., nutrients from food) and apply them in different cultures and representations. If Mr. Hewitt, after receiving feedback from his students, had not made this change, students might have responded with frustration by disengaging, not participating, or actively being off task. Such frustration means "I don't understand; I can't relate; I don't feel seen or heard in this lesson or these materials; I need this taught a different way."

Cultural influences come from family structures and affect many aspects of life. Cultural influences on socioecological and social determinants of health must not be ignored. Students have little control over where they live or what food is accessible at school, at home, and in the community. These factors may lead to food deserts and varied access to nutrient-dense foods. Health education teachers must not undermine the significance of these driving, persistent barriers. We have opportunities to value the diverse communities, cultures, food, and families of people of color, and we must use them to develop multiple narratives in our classes where all students feel seen and can see the diversity that brings value to our communities. Building connections at the surface level of observable cultures through food and holidays is the first step. Including diverse representation of foods and family structures in materials is another way to help students "see" themselves in health education class. Lastly, it is necessary to build in the deeper culture of how collectivist communities communicate and have values that may be different from those of individualist communities.

Discussion Questions

1. How does food affect the lives of the students you teach? What role did Mr. Hewitt play in bringing different voices and cultures into his lesson on food?

2. How essential are topics related to food justice, equity, and access to the planning of health education? Why is this important?

3. How can health education teachers learn from their students' cultural norms, traditions, and ethnic foods to elevate nutrient-dense foods from various cultures? And how can this knowledge be used to build an asset-based classroom where all cultures, foods, and family structures are represented and valued?

4. Why is it important to educate children about food deserts, food justice, social determinants of health, and socioecological models linked with poverty without putting down or harming students' cultural assets, influences, and environments that they have little control over?

5. Does your school district have a food policy? Does it align with messages shared here about cultural assets and nutrient-dense foods across different cultures of people of color and uplift all communities? How can you advocate to include such messages in your school's policy if they are not there and celebrate them if they are?

References and Suggested Resource

Baer-Sinott, S. "Food Is a Window to Cultural Diversity." 2020. *US News & World Report*, November 23, 2020. https://health.usnews.com/health-news/blogs/eat-run/articles/food-is-a-window-to-cultural-diversity.

Brooks, M. and D. Houck, eds. 2011. *The Speeches of Fannie Lou Hamer: To Tell It Like It Is*. Jackson, MS: University of Mississippi Press.

California Department of Education. n.d. "Culturally and Linguistically Responsive Teaching." California Department of Education." www.cde.ca.gov/pd/ee/responsiveteaching.asp.

Choi, A.S. 2014. "What Americans Can Learn From Other Food Cultures." Ideas.ted.com, December 18, 2014. https://ideas.ted.com/what-americans-can-learn-from-other-food-cultures/.

Colorado Department of Education. n.d. "Overview of Culturally Responsive Practices." In *High Impact Instructional Strategies for Health Education*. Colorado Department of Education. https://sitesed.cde.state.co.us/mod/book/view.php?id=8030&chapterid=8125.

"Food and Cooking: A Bridge to Cultural Understanding." n.d. Portland Community College Library website. www.pcc.edu/library/news/food-and-cooking-a-bridge-to-cultural-understanding/.

"Food: Food and Culture." n.d. Jrank. https://family.jrank.org/pages/639/Food-Food-Culture.html.

Hollie, S. 2019. "Branding Culturally Relevant Teaching: A Call for Remixes." *Teacher Education Quarterly* 46 (4): 31-52. www.jstor.org/stable/26841575.

Mingay, E., M. Hart, S. Yoong, and A. Hure. 2021. "Why We Eat the Way We Do: A Call to Consider Food Culture in Public Health Initiatives." *International Journal of Environmental Research and Public Health* 18 (22): 11967. www.ncbi.nlm.nih.gov/pmc/articles/PMC8623951/.

MSNBC. *Poor People's Campaign: A National Call for Moral Revival*. MSNBC, 2020.

Niccolls, K. 2020. "Creating Culturally Linguistic and Responsive Classrooms: A Place Where All Kids Belong." *Getting Smart*, February 11, 2020. www.gettingsmart.com/2020/02/11/creating-culturally-linguistic-and-responsive-class-rooms-a-place-where-all-kids-belong/.

Terry, B., ed. 2021. *Black Food: Stories, Art, And Recipes From Across The African Diaspora*. New York City: Penguin Random House.

CONCLUSION

Educators must be committed to creating learning spaces inclusive of all students and their families. The characteristics of white supremacy culture (see appendix A) serve as a barrier to exclude Black students from having access to and opportunities for advantages in society. If we are concerned about creating schools that work for Black students, we also must be willing to expand our definition of who's included in dominant society. It is also important to interrogate our behaviors to ensure that we are not replicating norms that exclude Black students from benefiting from the best the educational setting provides. Appendix B provides tips for creating your own case study.

Themes Presented

Intersectionality continues to bring to light more barriers for our students, compounding the levels of marginalized groups that one individual may have to navigate to access and apply health literacy skills. For example, a student may have multiple barriers, including being Black and also having a larger body size, experiencing mental health problems (like depression), being a lesbian, having a dark-skinned complexion, being an immigrant within the country, speaking another language as their first language, being of a lower socioeconomic status, and being homeless. Imagine identifying in some or all of these marginalized groups, and your teacher telling you to "just try harder" or "pull yourself up by your bootstraps" when you don't even own shoes that fit, metaphorically speaking. Systemic and institutional racism play into perpetuating the colonized ideals and mindsets, creating a constant struggle in how students in these marginalized groups navigate preK-12 school and how teachers can support them without doing more harm to them.

Key Takeaways

- Begin your equity and inclusion journey (or keep moving forward and reflecting on your EDI/equity journey).
- Be an advocate for change: Lift others (adults and children) up. Start where you are. Build a peer community. Create classroom norms and ground rules with and for your students.
- Continue to have difficult conversations.
- Be open to feedback and avoid sitting in comfort or being defensive when called out by the literature, peers, or students. (Know and unpack white supremacy culture ideals and learn how systemic and institutional racism will continue unless we dismantle it and serve our Black students.)
- Review class materials, curricula, and other student-facing materials to see if students see themselves. (Do your materials show a diverse population based on *all* marginalized groups? Do your outcomes and tasks lend themselves to students showing what they know in different ways that all meet grade-level outcomes and universal design for learning [UDL]?)
- Make sure health literacy skills and content include data of various marginalized groups.
- Review content from the viewpoint of including all communities in an asset-based rather than deficit-based mindset.
- Most importantly, take time to develop relationships and community with all students so that they feel comfortable speaking their truth, heard, and valued in the learning community.

Definitions

Anti-Blackness
Anti-Blackness refers to actions or behaviors that minimize, marginalize, or devalue the full participation of Black people in life (Weathersby 2019; Ross 2020). Specifically, it "describes the system of oppression that is based on institutional practices, policies, and cultural messages—as well as the beliefs held by and actions of individuals—to advantage one group over another and is used to oppress Black people" (Jackson 2022, 44).

Asset-Based Approaches
Asset-based approaches "utilize the strength and opportunities that the community provides rather than the problems or needs of the community" (Keratithamkul, Kim, and Roehrig 2020, 5).

Assimilation
Assimilation is when members from underrepresented groups reject or abdicate their core cultural practices and adopt others that are more widely accepted (Kim 2016; Racial Equity Tools 2022).

Bias
"Bias consists of attitudes, behaviors, and actions that are prejudiced in favor of or against one person or group compared to another" (NIH n.d.).

Black Joy
"[Black] Joy is defined as a feeling of great happiness and pleasure. [Black] Joy has also been described as divine purpose in action, paying homage to our ancestors, and the celebration of sacredness. Choosing joy in the face of oppression, violence, and global pandemonium can be viewed as resistance and self-care in current day." (Brooks 2020, 62).

Code-Switching
Code-switching is when a member in an underrepresented group recognizes the power dynamics in the more dominant group and consciously or subconsciously adjusts themselves (i.e., talk, behavior, appearance, dialect, etc.) to gain acceptance, access, or favor so that they can fit into these restrictive and oppressive environments (Doss and Gross 1994).

Colorblind Racism
"I don't see color" is a common statement that conceptualizes colorblind racism. By omitting race as a key factor, the individual perpetuates colorblind racism through acknowledging that racism does not exist.

Another way to state this is that someone is "blind," unable to see race, and is choosing not to see race or skin color and therefore also does not see racial disparities and institutional and systemic racism (Williams 2011).

Cultural Destructiveness
Cultural destructiveness is where the needs of a particular racial or cultural group are ignored, as opposed to cultural proficiency, where organizations respond effectively to the needs of diverse groups (Lindsey, Robins, and Terrel 2009).

Culture
Culture represents the accumulated histories, attitudes, behaviors, languages, values, beliefs, and uniqueness that distinguish subcultural groups in a society (Davis 2015; Kroeber and Kluckhohn 1952).

Critical Consciousness
Critical consciousness was developed by the Brazilian educator Paulo Freire in 2014 and is described as "an educational pedagogy to liberate the masses from systemic inequity maintained and perpetuated by process, practices, and outcomes of interdependent systems and institutions" (Jemal 2018).

Critical Race Theory
Critical race theory does the following:
1. Argues that racial inequity in education is linked to achievement and competition
2. Examines policies and practices that put forward white cultural norms and perpetuate racial inequity
3. Takes down both the negative narrative that Black people are inferior and white supremacy culture norms
4. Links historical progression leading to racism and oppression
5. Engages intersectional analysis and how race connects with other marginalized groups based on gender, immigration status, language, sexuality, and class
6. Advocates and creates discomfort in hopes of addressing racial inequity (Ladson-Billings and Tate 1995; Dixson and Anderson 2018)

Culturally Responsive Teaching
Culturally responsive teaching is "using the cultural knowledge, prior experiences, frames of reference, and performance styles of ethnically diverse students to make learning encounters more relevant to and effective for them." (Gay 2018, 36).

Cycle of Poverty
The cycle of poverty, which may also be called generational poverty, describes generations of living in low socioeconomic status (Noguera 2011; Payne 2005).

Deficit-Based Lens

A deficit-based lens is focused on the problem instead of on the potential for greatness. It is always thinking of your students, families, and communities as projects that need to be solved or fixed. It's shifting the discourse from individual outcomes to systemic barriers that were born from inequitable policies, practices, and, most importantly, deficit belief systems (Keratithamkul, Kim, and Roehrig 2020).

Health Disparities

Health disparities are "preventable differences in the burden of disease, injury, violence, or opportunities to achieve optimal health that are experienced by socially disadvantaged populations." (CDC 2023).

Implicit Bias

Also known as unconscious bias, "implicit bias is a form of bias that occurs automatically and unintentionally, that nevertheless affects judgments, decisions, and behaviors" (NIH n.d.).

Institutional Racism

Institutional Racism is societal allocation of privilege based on race (Hardeman et al. 2018). "Institutional racism refers to racially discriminatory policies and practices embedded in social institutions such as the government, the economy, the education system, the healthcare system, religious institutions, the family, and the media. Institutional racism is said to be systemic or structural when it operates as a system across multiple interconnected institutions" (Needham et al. 2022, 2).

Intersectionality

Intersectionality is a prism to see the interactive effects of various forms of discrimination and disempowerment. It looks at the way that racism, often, interacts with the patriarchalism, heterosexism, classism, and xenophobia and that the overlapping vulnerabilities created by these systems create specific challenges (Nast, 2018).

Microaggressions or Microinsults

Microaggressions or microinsults are intentional or unintentional, commonplace verbal, behavioral, or environmental indignities (Solorzano, Ceja, and Yosso 2000).

Othered or Othering

To other is to alienate a person or group. Examples include code-switching, microaggressions in teaching, examples of intersectionality through immigration status, and systems of oppression (Doss and Gross 1994).

Race

Race is defined by the United States Census Bureau as white, Black or African American, Asian, and Native Hawaiian or other Pacific Islander (United States Census Bureau 2022).

Racism
"Racism is a system—consisting of structures, policies, practices, and norms—that assigns value and determines opportunity based on the way people look or the color of their skin. This results in conditions that unfairly advantage some and disadvantage others throughout society" (CDC 2021).

Redlining
"Redlining can be defined as a discriminatory practice that consists of the systematic denial of services such as mortgages, insurance loans, and other financial services to residents of certain areas, based on their race or ethnicity. Redlining disregards individual's qualifications and creditworthiness to refuse such services, solely based on the residency of those individuals in minority neighborhoods; which were also quite often deemed 'hazardous' or 'dangerous.'" (Cornell Law School 2022).

Restorative Justice (in Education)
Restorative justice in education is a structure or process that empowers students to resolve their own conflicts. It also provides students with restorative practices like circles and mindfulness (Davis 2015).

SCARF Model
The SCARF model is a brain-based model for collaboration with others. It includes five domains that influence behaviors in social situations: status, certainty, autonomy, relatedness, and fairness (Rock 2008).

Social Determinants of Health
Social determinants of health include education, employment, health systems and services, housing, income and wealth, physical environment, public safety, social environment, and transportation (Baciu et al. 2017)

Socioecological Model
The socioecological model is used to reflect on systems, looking at how the individual is influenced or at the center with relationships, then community, and then within a society (Dahlberg and Krug 2002).

Structural Racism
Structural racism "refers to the totality of ways in which societies foster racial discrimination through mutually reinforcing systems of housing, education, employment, earnings, benefits, credit, media, health care and criminal justice. These patterns and practices in turn reinforce discriminatory beliefs, values and distribution of resources" (Bailey et al. 2017).

Systemic Racism
Systemic racism "emphasizes the involvement of whole systems, and often all systems—for example, political, legal, economic, health care, school, and criminal justice systems—including the structures that uphold the systems" (Bravemen et al. 2022).

Unconscious Bias or Implicit Bias
"Unconscious bias (also known as implicit bias) refers to unconscious forms of discrimination and stereotyping based on race, gender, sexuality, ethnicity, ability, age, and so on. It differs from cognitive bias, which is a predictable pattern of mental errors that result in us misperceiving reality and, as a result, deviating away from the most likely way of reaching our goals" (Tsipursky 2020).

White Cultural Norms/White Supremacy Culture
White cultural norms, or white supremacy culture, are characteristics, norms, and standards that promote and continue white dominant culture. White supremacy culture characteristic are as follows: perfectionism; sense of urgency; defensiveness; quantity over quality; worship of the written word; only one right way; paternalism; either-or thinking; power hoarding; fear of open conflict; individualism; I'm the only one; progress is bigger/more; objectivity; and right to comfort (Okun 1999; "Dismantling Racism: A Workbook for Social Change Groups" n.d.).

White Fragility
White fragility occurs when racial stress becomes triggering and intolerable, creating a range of defensive moves (DiAngelo 2011).

White Privilege
White privilege exists due to historical context. Health education examples include walking into a grocery store and seeing white hygiene products or white-flesh-colored bandages as the dominant option and a separate section for care of people of color (Collins 2018).

White Supremacy
White supremacy is "a form of racism centered upon the belief that white people are superior to people of other racial backgrounds and that whites should politically, economically, and socially dominate nonwhites. While often associated with violence perpetrated by the KKK and other white supremacist groups, it also describes a political ideology and systemic oppression that perpetuates and maintains the social, political, historical and/or industrial white domination" (NEA Center for Social Justice 2020).

References

Baciu, A., Y. Negussie, A. Geller, et al., eds. 2017. *National Academies of Sciences, Engineering, and Medicine; Health and Medicine Division; Board on Population Health and Public Health Practice; Committee on Community-Based Solutions to Promote Health Equity in the United States*. Washington, DC: National Academies Press.

Bailey, Z.D., N. Krieger, M. Agenor, J. Graves, N. Linos, and M.T. Bassett. 2017. "Structural Racism and Health Inequities in the USA: Evidence and Interventions." *Lancet* 389 (10077): 1453-1463. (Cited in AMA's "Prioritizing Equity: The Root Cause" video.)

Bravemen, P., E. Arkin, D. Proctor, T. Kauh, and N. Holm. 2022. "Systemic and Structural Racism: Definitions, Examples, Health Damages, and Approaches to Dismantling." *Health Affairs* 41 (2). www.healthaffairs.org/doi/10.1377/hlthaff.2021.01394.

Brooks, L.B. 2020. "Black Joy, Black Love and COVID-19: A Reflection on Self-Care and Community in the Midst of a Pandemic." *Journal of Black Sexuality and Relationships* 7(1): 67-72. https://doi.org/10.1353/bsr.2020.0012.

CDC (Centers for Disease Control and Prevention). 2021. "Racism and Health." Last modified November 24, 2021. www.cdc.gov/minorityhealth/racism-disparities/index.html.

CDC (Centers for Disease Control and Prevention). 2023. "Health Disparities." Last modified May 26, 2023. www.cdc.gov/healthyyouth/disparities/index.htm.

Collins, C. 2018. "What Is White Privilege, Really?" *Learning for Justice* 60 (Fall). www.learningforjustice.org/magazine/fall-2018/what-is-white-privilege-really.

Cornell Law School. 2022. "Redlining." Last modified April 2022. https://www.law.cornell.edu/wex/redlining.

Dahlberg, L.L., and E.G. Krug. 2002. "Violence: A Global Public Health Problem." In *World Report on Violence and Health*, edited by E. Krug, L.L. Dahlberg, J.A. Mercy, A.B. Zwi, and R. Lozano, 1-21. Geneva, Switzerland: World Health Organization.

Davis, M. 2015. "Restorative Justice: Resources for Schools." Edutopia, updated October 29, 2015. www.edutopia.org/blog/restorative-justice-resources-matt-davis.

DiAngelo, R. 2011. "White Fragility." *International Journal of Critical Pedagogy* 3 (3): 54-70.

Dismantling Racism (website). n.d. dRworksbook. www.dismantlingracism.org

Dixson, A.D., and C.R. Anderson. 2018. "Where Are We? Critical Race Theory in Education 20 Years Later." *Peabody Journal of Education* 93 (1): 121-131. https://doi.org/10.1080/0161956X.2017.1403194.

Doss, R.C., and A.M. Gross. 1994. "The Effects of Black English and Code-Switching on Intraracial Perceptions." *Journal of Black Psychology* 20(3): 282. https://doi.org/10.1177/00957984940203003.

Gay, G. 2018. *Culturally Responsive Teaching: Theory, Research, and Practice.* 3rd ed. New York: Teachers College Press, Columbia University.

Hardeman, R.R., K.A. Murphy, J. Karbeah, and K.B. Kozhimannil. 2018. "Naming Institutionalized Racism in the Public Health Literature: A Systematic Literature Review." *Public Health Reports* 133 (3): 240-249. https://doi.org/10.1177/0033354918760574.

Jackson, D. 2022. *Making Sense of Black Students' Figured Worlds of Race, Racism, Anti-Blackness, and Blackness. Research in the Teaching of English* 57 (1), 43-66. https://doi.org/10.58680/rte202232001

Jemal A. 2017. "Critical Consciousness: A Critique and Critical Analysis of the Literature." *Urban Rev* 49 (4):602-626. https://doi: 10.1007/s11256-017-0411-3.

Keratithamkul, K., J.N. Kim, and G.H. Roehrig. 2020. "Cultural Competence or Deficit-Based View? A Qualitative Approach to Understanding Middle School Students' Experience with Culturally Framed Engineering." *International Journal of STEM Education* 7 (26).

Kim, N.Y. 2016. "Critical Thoughts on Asian American Assimilation in the Whitening Literature." In *Contemporary Asian America: A Multidisciplinary Reader*, 3rd ed., edited by M. Zhou and A.C. Ocampo, 554-575. New York and London: NYU Press.

Kroeber, A.L., and C. Kluckhohn. 1952. Culture: a critical review of concepts and definitions. Papers. Peabody Museum of Archaeology & Ethnology. *Harvard University* 47 (1): viii, 223.

Ladson-Billings, G., and W. Tate IV. 1995. Toward a Critical Race Theory of Education. *Teachers College Record*, 97 (1).

Lindsey, R. B., K. Robins, and R.D. Terrell. 2009. *Cultural Proficiency: A Manual for School Leaders*. Thousand Oaks, CA: Corwin Press.

Nast, C. 2018. *Kimberlé Crenshaw and Lady Phyll Talk Intersectionality, Solidarity, and Self-Care*. https://www.them.us/story/kimberle-crenshaw-lady-phyll-intersectionality

NEA (National Education Association) Center for Social Justice. 2020. "White Supremacy Culture Resources." www.nea.org/resource-library/white-supremacy-culture-resources.

NIH (National Institutes of Health). n.d. "Implicit Bias." https://diversity.nih.gov/sociocultural-factors/implicit-bias.

Needham, B.L., T. Ali, K.L Allgood, A. Ro, J.L. Hirschtick, and N.L. Fleischer. 2022. "Institutional Racism and Health: a Framework for Conceptualization, Measurement, and Analysis." *Journal of Racial and Ethnic Health Disparities*, August 22, 2022. https://doi.org/10.1007/s40615-022-01381-9.

Noguera, P.A. 2011. "A Broader and Bolder Approach Uses Education to Break the Cycle of Poverty." *Phi Delta Kappan* 93 (3): 8-14. https://doi.org/10.1177/003172171109300303.

Okun, T. 1999. "White Supremacy Culture." dRworksbook. www.dismantlingracism.org/uploads/4/3/5/7/43579015/okun_-_white_sup_culture.pdf.

Payne, R. 2005. *A Framework for Understanding Poverty*. 4th rev. ed. Highlands, TX: aha! Process.

Racial Equity Tools. 2022. "Racial Equity Tools Glossary." RacialEquityTools.org. www.racialequitytools.org/glossary.

Rock, D. 2008. "SCARF: A Brain-Based Model for Collaborating With and Influencing Others," *Neuroleadership Journal* 1: 1-9.

Solorzano, D., M. Ceja, and T. Yosso. 2000. "Critical Race Theory, Racial Microaggressions, and Campus Racial Climate: The Experiences of African American College Students." *The Journal of Negro Education*, 69 (1/2), 60-73.

Tsipursky, G. 2020. "What Is Unconscious Bias (and How You Can Defeat It)." *Psychology Today*, July 13, 2020. www.psychologytoday.com/us/blog/intentional-insights/202007/what-is-unconscious-bias-and-how-you-can-defeat-it.

United States Census Bureau. 2022. "About the Topic of Race." Last modified March 1, 2022. www.census.gov/topics/population/race/about.html.

Williams, M. 2011. "Colorblind Ideology Is a Form of Racism." *Psychology Today*, December 27, 2011. https://www.psychologytoday.com/us/blog/culturally-speaking/201112/colorblind-ideology-is-form-racism.

Appendix A

Racism and White Supremacy Culture

Resolved, That the House of Representatives—

(1) supports the resolutions drafted, introduced, and adopted by cities and localities across the Nation declaring racism a public health crisis;

(2) declares racism a public health crisis in the United States; (117th Congress 2021).

The Centers for Disease Control and Prevention (CDC), the American Public Health Association, and many other agencies, including our Congress, have declared that racism is a public health crisis. The COVID-19 pandemic elevated disproportionate outcomes for communities of people of color, further emphasizing the disparity based on race in the United States (CDC 2021). These outcomes are derived from systemic and institutionalized racism inequities. Access to health care is a primary barrier for communities of people of color. Social determinants of health outcomes are defined by race (CDC 2022; Mendez et al. 2021; NACo 2021). The CDC (2022) revised race standards, identifying five categories for data on race: American Indian or Alaska Native, Asian, Black or African American, Native Hawaiian or other Pacific Islander, and white. According to the CDC, "Social determinants of health (SDOH) are the nonmedical factors that influence health outcomes. They are the conditions in which people are born, grow, work, live, and age, and the wider set of forces and systems shaping the conditions of daily life. These forces and systems include economic policies and systems, development agendas, social norms, social policies, racism, climate change, and political systems. Centers for Disease Control and Prevention (CDC) has adopted this SDOH definition from the World Health Organization" (CDC 2022).

It is imperative for health educators to identify the barriers to access for the community of people of color linked to how we teach and provide instruction on health care access and to address working assumptions of teachers in being culturally aware of these institutionalized and systemic barriers derived from centuries of oppression. Explicitly stated, "The origin of the United States includes colonization, genocide, and land theft from Indigenous communities as a result of white supremacy and structural racism. The trauma and oppression committed against Indigenous communities has implications for health and well-being" (Mendez et al. 2021).

In health education, mental and emotional health is a major component of instruction. Day-to-day interpersonal or personally mediated racism has been correlated with stress on the body of those affected, leading to dysregulation (Mendez et al. 2021). Further data links low birth weight, high infant mortality, diabetes, and other chronic diseases with the dysregulation (Mendez et al. 2021). In looking at the socioecological model, redlining and segregation has a direct impact on health care access and further equates to health inequities (Bailey et al. 2017). Since the deaths of George Floyd and Breonna Taylor, publicly naming racism as a public health crisis is one way systems are working to dismantle systemic and institutionalized racism and reduce health inequities based on race.

Cycle of Socialization and White Supremacy Culture

Beverly Daniel Tatum (2017) often uses the imagery of the moving walkway to describe the different ways in which we passively maintain, intentionally perpetuate, or interrupt racism. In the first category, we replicate racism whether we know it or not. Schools and classrooms are not exempt from replicating racism. We are all born into families that provide us with our first socialization, helping to shape how we see ourselves and others in the world. Our families affirm behaviors that align with their beliefs and social norms.

Our second socialization comes when we leave home and begin to attend institutions like schools, religious institutions, and other organizations where our identities may be affirmed or rejected. Black parents have high expectations for their children, telling us we can be anything we want if we work hard. They add that "you may not always get what you want, but you will learn from the journey." They also know that some people will block our success because of our skin color. During our second socialization at school, while many educators support our success, others do their best to break our spirits. The messages we receive from home help us navigate these spaces where authorities reject our identities, so we don't internalize the low expectations of others and keep our identities intact.

Our third socialization comes from the wider world: the people we meet and experiences we have that challenge and affirm some of these early messages. We may come to a place where we encounter people and events that make us question ourselves and our worldview. At this crossroads, individuals must decide to continue with their worldview or go in a new direction based on an expanded worldview. Fear, confusion, and insecurity are the primary reasons people do not broaden their worldviews. This could be fear of being shunned by their family or peer group. They may become confused and find it easier to maintain the status quo, or they may experience insecurity about who they are or their alignment to something outside of the way they were socialized and continue to go along to get along (Harro 2010).

As educators, we are socialized to see schools and schooling through how we were socialized and affirmed in this context. Many educators had great experiences in school, and we want to replicate those experiences for the students we teach. Others became teachers because they did not have great experiences or did not have a role model who looked like them. The experiences of our students may be very different from our experiences, which may challenge our worldviews. We have to decide to maintain the current state, which may or may not work for our students, or to go in a new direction to improve outcomes for our Black students.

The cycle of socialization highlights how we can maintain the status quo and presents us with opportunities to disrupt worldviews that limit our beliefs, attitudes, and actions. The cycle of socialization also serves as a framework for understanding how white supremacy or dominant culture is replicated in our country. White supremacy culture operates hidden in the background as the norms we are expected to follow. In their seminal work *Dismantling Racism: A Workbook for Social Change Groups,* Jones and Okun (2001) identified the characteristics of white supremacy culture.

Characteristics of White Supremacy Culture

- Perfectionism
- Sense of urgency
- Defensiveness
- Quantity over quality
- Worship of the written word
- Paternalism
- Either-or thinking
- Power hoarding
- Fear of open conflict
- Individualism
- Progress is bigger/more
- Objectivity
- Right to comfort

The table below presents the characteristics of white supremacy culture paired with examples of how educators can interrupt these patterns with more inclusive practices.

Characteristic of white supremacy culture	How to interrupt White supremacy culture	How to push back against white supremacy culture using health education
Perfectionism	Model that mistakes are opportunities for growth.	· Provide students opportunities to grow through an iterative approach or scaffolded design for learning. · Provide feedback that highlights what is going well as well as critical growth areas.
Sense of urgency	· Be realistic about the length of time instructional materials and tasks will take. · Take the time to build relational trust and a positive class climate.	· Set ground rules or agreed-upon procedures for learning. · Review decision-making and goal-setting health literacy skills to guide the process. · Focus on being realistic and checking for progress and short-term goals prior to the long-term goal. · Identify possible barriers and key partners in the plan.
Defensiveness	· Teacher to teacher: Be open to develop new ideas and instructional strategies. · Teacher to student(s): Be open to all as assets in the instructional setting. Do not be defensive in feeling that your "position of power" as an adult or educator is being usurped.	In setting ground rules and goals and making decisions, consider ways that defensiveness may be elevated and how to work through teacher roles in facilitating instruction and student roles as assets to learning.
Quantity over quality	Avoid focusing on the test and focus on the process.	· Focus on student development of health literacy skills applied to different content topics. · Focus on the application of the health literacy skills and not on the total amount of work being done. · Provide multiple and varied ways for students to illustrate working toward the health education grade level outcomes.

Characteristic of white supremacy culture	How to interrupt White supremacy culture	How to push back against white supremacy culture using health education
Worship of the written word	· Avoid focusing on one right way to do things. · Teacher: Be open to accepting challenges from students that align to the goal or outcome. · Student(s): Be open to sharing, thinking, and speaking ideas honestly and reflectively without feeling that you will be punished.	· Be open to creativity and thinking that is different and may go beyond the test, assessment, or "rubric." · In establishing goals and making decisions, recognize and name with students that there are many correct ways to get to a common goal.
Paternalism	· Teacher: Realize you are in a position to empower your students. · Student(s): Know that teachers have the ability to be an advocate and control the learning environment.	· Facilitate and empower students to use decision-making health literacy skills to practice self-management and advocate for self and others. · Develop opportunities for students to see themselves in a "position of power" and have a voice in the classroom. · Share when you make a mistake or model practices.
Either-or thinking	Understand that focusing on one way or the other limits worldview outside of your own narrative.	· Use and practice interpersonal communication skills to acknowledge when you feel rushed into making an immediate "either-or" decision. · Deescalate the need to rush through a decision, and create different opportunities.
Power hoarding	"Those in power don't see themselves as hoarding power." Be aware you are taking power from others.	· Focus on health literacy skills to analyze the influences on power hoarding in a given context. · Create opportunities for students to practice scenarios that use interpersonal communication to resolve various conflicts across health education content areas.

(continued)

Characteristic of white supremacy culture	How to interrupt White supremacy culture	How to push back against white supremacy culture using health education
Fear of open conflict	· Agree to various perspectives in the classroom to avoid an emphasis on being "polite." · Do not cast negativity upon or name as being insubordinate to the teacher, rude, or disruptive to the class environment those who bring up difficult issues.	· Practice interpersonal communication skills on critical thinking scenarios in health education. · Have students take two different views on the same topic and access valid and reliable information to support their views. · Create practices that can be normalized when students feel uncomfortable (for example, raise a hand, say ouch).
Individualism	Shift the focus from competition and achievement over others to collectivism and group learning.	· Create a more collectivist project, construct, or aim in class projects focused on teamwork and collaboration. · Emphasize the collective goal of students being able to know and practice health literacy skills now and in the future to maintain quality of life and advocate for self and others.
Progress is bigger/more	Believe the more we have, the better.	· Identify assessment plans and goals for the health education class, giving students access to multiple ways to show what they know, with a focus on proficiency in one as opposed to completion of all assignments. · Focus on the assignment components that show growth or meet standards; focus on quality over quantity. · Provide choice in assessment that is linked to common outcomes for health education (e.g., social media campaign, slides, pamphlet, poster board project, writing a paper, poem, music).
Objectivity	Invite and include multiple voices and perspectives from marginalized groups (see figure P.1).	· Include opportunities for students to show their passion and emotions linked to mental and emotional health and well-being and interpersonal communication throughout the course, not just in that unit. · Acknowledge emotions and affirm all voices.

Characteristic of white supremacy culture	How to interrupt White supremacy culture	How to push back against white supremacy culture using health education
Right to comfort	Do not take things personally to sit in comfort (e.g., not taking a stand because that would make others feel uncomfortable) when being questioned, unpacking confusion on a task or content, or hearing opinions in a given health topic.	· Provide opportunities for multiple viewpoints to be presented through accessing valid and reliable information. · Acknowledge and name that change theory shows that great discomfort occurs prior to getting through the change—or the "storm" comes before you "norm" the culture.

Adapted by permission from T. Okun, "White Supremacy Culture - Still Here," last modified August 2023, https://www.whitesupremacyculture.info/.

References and Suggested Resources

117th Congress. 2021. H. RES. 344, introduced in House April 22, 2021. www.congress.gov/bill/117th-congress/house-resolution/344/text.

American Public Health Association. n.d. "Racism Is a Public Health Crisis." Accessed February 2023. www.apha.org/topics-and-issues/health-equity/racism-and-health/racism-declarations.

American Public Health Association. 2020. "Racism Is an Ongoing Public Health Crisis That Needs Our Attention Now." Press release, May 29, 2020. www.apha.org/news-and-media/news-releases/apha-news-releases/2020/racism-is-a-public-health-crisis.

Bailey, Z.D., N. Krieger, M. Agénor, J. Graves, N. Linos, and M.T. Bassett. 2017. "Structural Racism and Health Inequities in the USA: Evidence and Interventions." *Lancet* 389: 1453-63.

Bryant, B., and S. Gimont. 2021. "CDC Declares Racism a Public Health Threat." NACo, April 8, 2021. www.naco.org/blog/cdc-declares-racism-serious-public-health-threat.

CDC (Centers for Disease Control and Prevention). 2021. "Racism and Health." Last modified November 24, 2021. www.cdc.gov/minorityhealth/racism-disparities/index.html.

CDC (Centers for Disease Control and Prevention). 2022. "Social Determinants of Health at CDC." Last modified December 8, 2022. www.cdc.gov/about/sdoh/index.html.

Cornell Health. "Racism as a Public Health Crisis." n.d. February, 2023. https://health.cornell.edu/initiatives/skorton-center/racism-public-health-crisis.

Harro, B. 2010. "The Cycle of Socialization." *Sticks & Stones: Understanding Implicit Bias, Microaggressions, and Stereotypes*. National Educator Association Center for Social Justice. www.nea.org/sites/default/files/2021-02/Cycle%20of%20Socialization%20HARRO.pdf.

Harvard T. H. Chan School of Public Health. 2020. "Why Declaring Racism a Public Health Crisis Matters." www.hsph.harvard.edu/news/hsph-in-the-news/racism-public-health-crisis-bassett/.

Jones, K., and T. Okun. 2001. "White Supremacy Culture, a Summary." From *Dismantling Racism: A Workbook for Social Change Groups.* Chapel Hill, NC: Oak Consulting. www.berkeleypublicschoolsfund.org/wp-content/uploads/2020/07/White-Supremacy-Culture-Summary.pdf.

Mendez, D.D., J. Scott, L. Adodoadji, C. Toval, M. McNeil, and M. Sindhu. 2021. "Racism as Public Health Crisis: Assessment and Review of Municipal Declarations and Resolutions Across the United States." *Frontiers in Public Health* 9:686807. https://doi.org/10.3389/fpubh.2021.686807.

NACo (National Association of Counties). 2021. "NACo American County Platform and Resolutions 2020-2021." Washington, DC: NACo. www.naco.org/sites/default/files/documents/Health%202020-2021%20American%20County%20Platform%203.23.21.pdf.

Paradies, Y.C. 2006. "Defining, Conceptualizing and Characterizing Racism in Health Research." *Critical Public Health* 16:143-57. https://doi.org/10.1080/09581590600828881.

Tatum, B. 2017. *Why Are All the Black Kids Sitting Together in the Cafeteria?: And Other Conversations About Race.* New York City: Basic Books.

Vestal, C. 2020. "Racism Is a Public Health Crisis, Say Cities and Counties." *Stateline*, June 15, 2020. www.pewtrusts.org/en/research-and-analysis/blogs/stateline/2020/06/15/racism-is-a-public-health-crisis-say-cities-and-counties.

Appendix B
Building Your Own Case Study

To further develop and critically think through health education intersectionality, students in this course can create their own case studies based on the following scenarios. This permits reflecting on and elevating different viewpoints that can further elevate institutionalized and systemic racism, ableism, homophobia, xenophobia, and other biases against marginalized groups of people. Additionally, creating case studies provides opportunities for the reader to apply health literacy skills through interpersonal communication, decision-making, goal setting, analyzing influences, accessing valid and reliable information, self-management, and advocacy through the development and application of research in case study design. These are some sample scenarios:

- Students are grouped by gender for family life and human sexuality lessons. Transgender and nonbinary students are placed in their group by their gender assigned at birth.

- In reviewing your health education classes, you see that none of the students in one class have languages other than English as their first language.

- In your team review of interims or grades, you discuss disaggregated data by free and reduced meals (lower socioeconomic status), racial subgroups, special education status, gender, and English as a second language–identified students. One of your teammates has over 45 percent of students failing the health education class. When looking further, you find that all the failing students are in one of these subgroups.

- Black and Brown students are treated differently in a health education class because they cannot "be quiet" while the teacher is lecturing and they get "too loud" during group work. They are "out of control."

- During a nutrition and fitness lesson, the teacher introduces body mass index (BMI) and shares that this is the "healthy" weight for individuals. She looks at students who are "overweight" when talking about the need for better nutrition and exercise to get weight under control. The health teacher also uses white or Eurocentric beauty images as guidance for the way people should look.

Building Your Own Case Study

The goal of case studies is to provide an opportunity to look at a scenario or situation with the goal of observing and analyzing behaviors; reviewing theory and practices; and analyzing, problem solving and promoting discussion on a given topic (Stake 1995; Yin 1984). Gorski and Pothini (2018) highlight explicit ways to develop case studies that elevate racially and otherwise marginalized groups of people through an equity and social justice focus.

Tips for Writing a Case Study

1. What is the problem to be solved? Identify the issues or problems. Explicitly name the marginalized group or groups and the issue linked. These can build on real-life scenarios. Consider biases, micro-aggressions, assumptions, stereotypes, and instructional practices that can limit or uplift a small population while negating others.

2. Research and collect information on the topic. Describe the context for learning population, teacher background, student background, socioeconomic status, race, gender, ability, and other aspects referenced within intersectionality. Give context for the timing of the case.

3. Develop your story or narrative. What perspectives are you looking to share? Be sure to share multiple perspectives and viewpoints.

4. Articulate your point and teaching outcome clearly using multiple examples in the case developed.

5. Identify areas for growth areas and successes elevated in the case.

6. Connect the case with research, theory, and citations with the goal of developing possible short- or long-term plans to apply within instructional practices and personal belief systems.

Adapted from Blackshear and Culp (2023), and Gorski and Pothini (2018).

References

Blackshear, T., and B. Culp. 2023. *Critical Race Studies in Physical Education.* Champaign, IL: Human Kinetics.

Gorski, P., and S. Pothini. 2018. *Case Studies on Diversity and Social Justice Education.* 2nd ed. New York: Routledge.

Stake, R. 1995. *The Art of Case Research.* Thousand Oaks, CA: Sage.

Yin, R. 1984. *Case Study Research: Design and Methods.* 1st ed. Beverly Hills, CA: Sage.

About the Authors

Cara D. Grant, EdD, is the preK-12 health and physical education supervisor in a large Maryland school district. She is also a lecturer in the department of kinesiology and is the MCERT (master of education with certification) professional development schools coordinator with the College of Education. Grant earned her undergraduate degree from the University of Maryland–College Park; a master's degree in secondary education, with a specialization in curriculum and instruction, from Bowie State University; and a doctorate in educational leadership from the University of Phoenix. She has worked in education, curriculum development, and teacher professional development for over 20 years in preK-12 education and for more than 4 years in higher education. She is a board member for the Society of Health and Physical Educators of Maryland (SHAPE Maryland) and serves as the chair for the Maryland State Department of Education Advisory Council on Health and Physical Education. She also serves on SHAPE America's board of directors and is the SHAPE America president-elect.

Troy E. Boddy, DOL, is the retired director of equity initiatives for Montgomery County Public Schools in Rockville, Maryland. In this role, he and his team were responsible for supporting the development practices, policies, and procedures that create access, opportunities to learn, and equitable academic and social-emotional outcomes for underserved students. He has coordinated the design and delivery of 27 equity training modules that build the awareness, knowledge, and skills necessary to ensure schools create the conditions needed to produce equitable outcomes for student achievement and success. Additionally, Boddy is the cofounder of Student Equity Advocates and the Building Our Network of Diversity (BOND) Project. He is the codirector of the Sandy Spring Slave

Museum, where he leads educational programs and professional learning. His publications include contributions to a case study for Life Case Studies for Inclusive Educators (2018) and Grandpa's River, a computer-integrated cross-curricular simulation (2001). Boddy is currently the president of the East Coast Racial Equity Group and provides consulting services to companies, schools, and community organizations on the subject of addressing equity and creating equitable workplaces.

About the Contributors

Daryl C. Howard, PhD, (he/him) is an equity instructional specialist whose work and research interests include race and cultural proficiency, social-emotional learning, and the triumphs and challenges of African American male students. As chair of Maryland's State Department of Education's Advisory Council on Equity and Excellence for Black Boys, he researches and recommends policy and practice to disrupt harmful narratives, decrease disproportionality, and elevate  achievement. Dr. Howard is instrumental in the work of the Building Our Network of Diversity (BOND) Project, where he leads initiatives focused on the recruitment, development, and retention of male educators of color, as well as empowerment of underserved male students. Dr. Howard lectures on the topics of race, sociology, and education at McDaniel College and Prince George's Community College and is the author of *Complex People: Insights at the Intersection of Black Culture and American Social Life*. Lastly, Dr. Howard is part of the NEA Foundation's Educators' Table, a program that seeks to uplift the voices of outstanding educators on key issues, including equity, educational justice, and workforce diversity.

Deanna Toler Kuhney, MA, (she/her) is a racial equity educator, trainer, and facilitator. She is especially skilled in creating and facilitating "safer" spaces, which enable participants to engage in courageous conversations around race, racism, equity, and inclusion. Ms. Kuhney is currently codeveloping a curriculum for Black high school girls and school leaders. She has worked with school systems, nonprofits, and private  organizations for the past 20 years. Some of her work has been for districts in Maryland; Connecticut; Washington, D.C.; and Vermont. She has enjoyed working throughout a variety of industries, from the arts to professional learning. Ms. Kuhney holds a bachelor of business administration degree from Pace University, a master's degree in contemporary communications from Notre Dame of Maryland University, and a postgraduate certificate in educational equity from McDaniel College. She currently resides in Silver Spring, Maryland, and enjoys spending time with her children and grandchildren, riding her motorcycle, and taking weekend trips to Ocean City to work on her 1954 trailer. She is also a member of Delta Sigma Theta Sorority.

Patricia Morgan, PhD, (she/her) is an innovative and passionate leader with a heart for equity, access, inclusion, and social justice. She serves as the chief executive officer and founder of the Executive Learning Lab and specializes in organizational development and sustainable change. Her experience includes being a secondary teacher; a K-12 science, health, and physical education system administrator; a part-time university instructor; and an international consultant. She has  written several publications about culturally responsive organizations, critical consciousness, and access and barriers to justice. She has conducted numerous studies and presentations on these topics at local, national, and international conferences. She has also hosted several keynotes and plenary sessions for educational, for-profit, and nonprofit organizations through her consulting firm. Dr. Morgan has earned degrees from the University of Miami and Georgia State University.

Tiffany Monique Quash, PhD, (she/her) is the qualitative/survey research methodologist for American University. She received her bachelor's degree from Randolph-Macon Woman's College in political science with a minor in African studies; master of education degree from Springfield College in physical education with a minor in athletic administration; and doctorate from the Indiana University School of Public Health in leisure behavior with a minor in higher education.  Dr. Quash taught sexual education for Springfield (Massachusetts) Public Schools and has coached swimming for several years in Massachusetts, California, and Washington, D.C. In 2019, she delivered a TEDx talk titled "Learning to Swim Is a Human Right," which is solution-focused to addressing the racial drowning disparity while celebrating the success of Black womxn swimmers. In 2023, Dr. Quash contributed to the text *Critical Race Studies in Physical Education* by writing the chapters "Case Study 3: Gendered Racism, Racial Disparities, and the Black Body" and "Case Study 7: More Than a Bathroom: Black Transgender Student." Dr. Quash resides in Virginia with her wife, Tasha.

Victor Ramsey, EdD, (he/him) is an adjunct assistant professor in the department of health and human performance at York College, City University of New York, where he teaches undergraduate courses in health and physical education. He retired in 2022 after three decades in the New York City Department of Education teaching health and physical education and subsequently becoming an educational administrator

with the Office of School Wellness Programs. Here he provided support for health and physical instruction and trainings to health and physical education educators throughout New York City. He is currently a member of the board of directors of SHAPE America and the New York State Association for Health, Physical Education, Recreation and Dance. In the latter, he was the recipient of the 2022 Distinguished Service Award. He is also an active member of American Educational Research Association Special Interest Group 93.

Brendan Joseph Tassy, MEd, (he/him) is a health and wellness educator at Springfield College, where he has spent the last four semesters teaching health and wellness courses while completing his master of education degree in health promotion and disease prevention. Mr. Tassy completed his undergraduate degree at Springfield College with a major in movement and sports studies with a concentration in physical education and a minor in coaching. In his young education career, he views these degrees as his greatest accomplishments thus far. Mr. Tassy's impact on education has been recognized by MAHPERD through the MAHPERD Outstanding Future Professional Award. He aims to have a positive impact on all his students, promoting lifelong health and wellness through spirit, mind, and body.

Anika Thrower, PhD, (she/her) earned her bachelor of science degree in consumer science and nutrition from Norfolk State University in 2001. She earned both her master of public health degree and doctorate in public health and community health from Walden University. As a health practitioner, Dr. Thrower served in Women, Infants and Children's (WIC) programs around the United States for over 16 years; her most rewarding experience was serving at a Native American community in Washington State. She is a seasoned researcher, having published several peer-reviewed scholarly articles. In 2013, Dr. Thrower won the Presidential Alumni Research Dissemination Award from Walden University. A professor at the Borough of Manhattan Community College, she teaches community health courses rooted in culturally responsive pedagogy. Dr. Thrower's research interests include addressing the college enrollment crisis, gaps in higher education attainment, and collaborative learning pedagogies. She is the principal coeditor of an upcoming book, *Autoethnographic Approaches to Addressing the College Enrollment Crisis*. Dr. Thrower's most recent book chapter was "A Black Scholar's Trek to Higher Ground: The Dance" in *Black Women Navigating Historically White Higher Education Institutions and the Journey Toward Liberation* (2022).

Porsche Vanderhorst, MEd, (she/her) is the founder and owner of an educational consulting firm focusing on nurturing joy and justice in education. She has spent a decade supporting school and system administrators, teachers, staff, students, families, and communities in examining how race and culture impact teaching, learning, leading, and relationships. As an educator for over 15 years, she has served as a classroom teacher, an equity instructional specialist, a learning and achievement specialist for school improvement, and an assistant principal. She passionately cultivates safe, joyful, and fruitful communities for adult learning and advocacy while also maintaining relationships with students through mentoring and putting herself in positions where she can intentionally learn from the genius of children, youth, and young adults. Ms. Vanderhorst holds a bachelor of science degree in English language arts education from Oakwood College (now University), a master of education degree in secondary curriculum and instruction from Howard University, and certifications in equity and excellence in education and administration from McDaniel College and in justice from HarvardX. She believes with all her heart, mind, and soul that "the time is always right to do what is right" (Dr. Martin Luther King Jr., 1967) and that where there is life, there is hope.

About SHAPE America

SHAPE
America

SOCIETY
OF HEALTH
AND PHYSICAL
EDUCATORS®

health. moves. minds.

SHAPE America – Society of Health and Physical Educators serves as the voice for 200,000+ health and physical education professionals across the United States. The organization's extensive community includes a diverse membership of health and physical educators, as well as advocates, supporters, and 50+ state affiliate organizations.

Since its founding in 1885, the organization has defined excellence in physical education. For decades, SHAPE America's National Standards for K-12 Physical Education have served as the foundation for well-designed physical education programs across the country. Additionally, the organization helped develop and owns the National Health Education Standards.

SHAPE America provides programs, resources, and advocacy that support an inclusive, active, and healthier school culture, and the organization's newest program—health. moves. minds.©—helps teachers and schools incorporate social and emotional learning so students can thrive physically and emotionally.

Our Vision

A nation where all children are prepared to lead healthy, physically active lives.

Our Mission

To advance professional practice and promote research related to health and physical education, physical activity, dance, and sport.

To learn more, visit **www.shapeamerica.org**.